BIG BOOK
of
Object Talks

David C Cook®
transforming lives together

www.davidccook.com

BIG BOOK OF OBJECT TALKS FOR KIDS OF ALL AGES
Published by David C Cook
4050 Lee Vance Drive
Colorado Springs, CO 80918 U.S.A.

David C Cook U.K., Kingsway Communications
Eastbourne, East Sussex BN23 6NT, England

ISBN 978-0-8307-7238-4

This content included in this book was originally published as *Really Big Book of Kids Sermons and Object Talks*
by Gospel Light in 2004 © Gospel Light, ISBN 978-0-8307-3657-3.

Cover Design: James Hershberger

Printed in the United States of America

1 2 3 4 5 6 7 8 9 10

082718

Contents

Jesus

Love for Others

Love from God

Obeying God

Peace

Praise and Worship

Prayer

Salvation

Service to Others

Thankfulness

Tips

Object talks can draw children in and help them apply the Bible truths to their lives. These object talks can be used as family devotions, children's sermons, or supplements to any Sunday school curriculum. They can also augment any children's ministry program, day school, or homeschool curriculum.

Getting the Most Out of an Object Talk

Preparation is the key to using *Big Book of Object Talks for Kids of All Ages*. Read a talk at least several days ahead to give ample time to gather the needed materials. You may find it helpful to practice some talks before presenting them.

Whenever possible, invite children to participate. Each time you present an object talk, ask a different child to read the Bible verse aloud.

Occasionally describe situations in which knowing God's Word has helped you. Tell children how the Bible verse presented in the object talk has been important to you.

Suggestions for Using the Object Talks

- **Adult Worship Service**—If the children in your church are in some or all of the adult service, consider using the object talk as the basis for a weekly children's sermon.
- **Newsletter**—Encourage parents to use the object talk with their children. To support your church's parents in their significant job of teaching Bible truths to their children, insert the object talk into a family newsletter you send every month.

- **Website**—Instead of or in addition to a newsletter, post on your church's website an object talk every week or month for families to access and use for family devotions.
- **Parenting Classes**—Distribute copies of selected object talks as part of classes on parenting and invite parents to use the object talks at home. Each object talk discusses a topic important to families, such as service to others ("School Uniforms"), obeying God ("Rainbow Fun"), and forgiving others ("'Awe'some Forgiveness").
- **Holidays**—Combine Christmas and Easter object talks into a separate pamphlet and distribute to families to help them keep children focused on the biblical truths of these holidays.
- **Program Resources**—Provide copies of object talks to leaders and teachers to use in supplementing their curriculums.
- **School Resources**—Provide copies of object talks to teachers in weekday school or to parents who homeschool their children.

Leading a Good Discussion

A good discussion requires leaders to listen as much as—or more than—they speak. However, encouraging others to speak up can be difficult. The following questions are commonly asked about making a discussion truly productive, and not an unfocused, rambling monologue.

How do I keep the discussion on track?

Use the discussion questions provided with each object talk to focus on children's personal experiences. When Bible truths relate to daily life, interest in the discussion will grow.

How do I get the discussion back on track if a digression occurs?

If significant interest is shown in the new topic and it has real value—and if you feel able to guide this new topic for discussion—then you may decide to stay with the new issue. Otherwise, use questions to bring attention back to the original topic. Move on to a new question, restate your question, or rephrase your question if the group did not understand what you asked.

If an outside interruption catches the group's attention, acknowledge it as matter-of-factly as possible, and then restate the question being discussed. You may also want to summarize some of the key points already made in the discussion.

What do I do when no one says anything or when kids are giving pat answers?

If you've asked a thought-provoking question, assume kids need at least a few moments to think. Be silent for a bit (no more than 20 to 30 seconds), and repeat or rephrase the question. If you still get no response, give your own answer to the question and move on.

If silence is a recurring problem, evaluate the questions you ask. Are they too vague? Are they too threatening? Do they require knowledge the kids do not have? Are the answers too obvious?

If the questions are fine, evaluate your response to what the group says. Are you unwilling to accept answers if they differ from what you consider to be the correct responses? Do you tend to always improve the students' answers? Work to create a climate of openness and trust.

Finally, add some variety to your approach in asking questions:

- Have students write their answers on paper. This allows them time to organize their thoughts. Then invite them to read what they wrote.
- Divide the class into smaller groups. You may ask all groups the same questions or assign different questions to each group. Invite volunteers to share the answers for their groups.

The same suggestions apply when students are giving only pat answers. The root problem is often the same in either case: the discussion participants do not feel secure sharing what they really think.

Leading a Child to Christ

One of the greatest privileges of serving in children's ministry is to help guide children to become members of God's family. Pray and ask God to prepare the kids you know to understand and receive the good news about Jesus. Ask God to give you the sensitivity and wisdom to communicate effectively and to be aware as opportunities occur.

When talking with children about salvation, use words and phrases they understand; never assume kids understand a concept just because they can repeat certain words. Avoid symbolic terms that will confuse literal-minded thinkers. As you watch and pray, you will see kids developing relationships with God.

Here are some questions you can ask and things you can discuss with a child who is interested in accepting Jesus as their Lord and Savior. Encourage the child to look up and read the Bible verses along with you.

Read John 3:16. **Why did God send Jesus to earth?** (God loved us so much that He wants us to have eternal life with Him.)

First John 3:1 says that God wants us to be His children. But sin, doing wrong, separates us from God. Read Romans 6:23. **What do you think should happen to us when we sin?** (die) **But what is God's gift to us?** (eternal life in Jesus)

Jesus willingly died on the cross to take the punishment for our sins. Read 1 Corinthians 15:3. **But Jesus didn't stay in the tomb. After three days, He came back to life! Jesus died so that we can live forever in heaven with Him.**

Are you sorry for the wrong things that you've done? If you are, what should you do? Read 1 John 1:9. **Our sins are wiped away when we're truly sorry for what we've done and when we turn to God.**

Read Ephesians 2:8. **How are we saved?** (by God's grace, through faith) **Christian faith is a life-long adventure here on earth. With Jesus as Lord of our lives, we build a life of submitting to God, following Jesus, and keeping in step with the Spirit.**

At this point, continue to talk with the child about accepting Jesus as Lord and Savior. Include what your church teaches about how this happens. If you have any questions about salvation, talk with your pastor or children's ministry leader.

God wants every person to accept the free gift of eternal life that He's offering. What do you need to do about this?

Encouragement

Lighting the Way
God gives us courage in all situations.

**Be strong and courageous....
Do not be discouraged, for
the LORD your God will be
with you wherever you go.**

Joshua 1:9

Materials
- Bible with bookmarks at Joshua 1:9 and Psalm 59:16–17
- object(s) used in dark areas (night-light, flashlight, candle, lantern, etc.)
- paper, pencils *(optional)*

Introduction
In all situations, we can count on God to give us the courage we need. Let's look at some things people might use at times when they are scared.

Presentation

1. Display the object(s) you brought. **What is this? When do people use it? How does it help them?** Volunteers can respond. **Sometimes people use these kinds of lights when it's dark. They might need to see where they are going, or maybe they just want to see the light because it makes them feel safe. What are some things younger kids might use to help them feel safe when it's dark?**

2. **When David, the man in Bible times who eventually became king of Israel, wanted to feel safe, he depended on God to give him courage. David wrote several psalms about times he needed courage. Psalm 59 is a psalm David wrote when Saul wanted to kill him.** Read or ask an older child to read Psalm 59:16–17 aloud. **Writing and singing this psalm must have helped David remember and celebrate God's help and care for him, because David wrote other psalms at other scary times in his life.**

Conclusion
Just as David trusted God to give him courage, we can also count on God to give us courage in all the situations we face. Read Joshua 1:9 aloud. **Just knowing God is with us wherever we go gives us all the courage we need!** Pray, thanking God for His gift of courage and that He is with us wherever we go.

Discussion Questions

1. **What does it mean to have courage?** (to do what is right even when it is hard or we feel afraid)

2. **When are times kids your age need courage?** (taking a test at school, performing in a music recital or acting in a play, being around older kids who are mean)

3. **What can we do to get courage in hard situations?** (pray to God, remember God's promise to be with us everywhere we go)

4. **Why can we always depend on receiving courage from God when we ask for it?** (God always keeps His promises.)

Additional Information for Older Children

In many Bibles, the word *miktam* is written under the title of Psalm 59. No one knows exactly what this word means. Some people think it was a word that described the kind of words David was writing or the melody to which the words were sung. *Miktam* is written under the titles of all the psalms David wrote when he was in great danger. *(Optional: Children can look at Psalms 56–60.)* Since *miktam* is only written under the psalms David wrote when he was in danger, what do you think the word might have meant?

Mirror Talk
No matter how bad it looks, God is with us.

Materials
- Bible with a bookmark at Psalm 118:6–7
- hand mirrors
- paper on which you have printed the sentence "The Lord is with me" backwards (see sketch)
- paper
- pencils

> **The LORD is with me;**
> **I will not be afraid.**
> **What can mere mortals**
> **do to me? The LORD is**
> **with me; he is my helper.**
> Psalm 118:6–7

Introduction
Because He promises to be with us, God can help us even when we're worried or afraid. Look at these words and see if you can figure out what they say and how God helps us in difficult times.

Presentation
1. In class, show the words you printed to one or more volunteers and ask them to try to read the words. **How hard is it to read these words? Why don't they make sense when you first look at them?**

2. Hold the words up to a mirror and invite several volunteers to read the words. Volunteers can write the sentence backwards and use mirrors to read the words.

ɘmʜɈiwƨibɿo⅃ɘʜT

Conclusion
Sometimes we might feel like all the wrong things are happening to us. We might feel like we can't understand why sad things happen to us or to others. But if we remember that God is with us, we can ask Him to help us **know what to do.** Read Psalm 118:6–7 aloud. Thank God for promising to be with us even in difficult times.

Discussion Questions

1. **When is a time kids your age might feel afraid or worried?**

2. **What are some of the ways God helps us?** (He gives us parents and friends and promises to hear and answer our prayers.)

3. **What other promises does God give us?** (to forgive us when we do wrong, to give us courage)

Mission Impossible?
God encourages us when we're afraid.

Materials
- Bible with a bookmark at Joshua 1:9
- 8½" x 11" paper
- scissors

Preparation
Practice cutting paper, following the directions below.

Introduction
**God gives us courage, even when we have something really hard to do.
Look at this impossible task with me!**

Presentation
1. Show paper and ask, **How might I fit my whole body
   through this paper?**

2. After children Conclusion that the task is impossible, fold
   the paper lengthwise. Cut the paper as shown (sketch
   a), making an uneven number of cuts approximately ½"
   apart. Cut on the fold between the first and last sections as
   shown (sketch b). Then carefully open up the folds and step
   through the circle you have made.

a.

b.

Do not cut.

cut

Do not cut.

Conclusion
**When something seems too hard to do or we're discouraged,
God can help us by giving us courage and helping us know what
to do. What does God promise to do?** Read Joshua 1:9 aloud. Thank
God for encouraging us when we're afraid.

Discussion Questions

1. **What might make a kid your age feel discouraged or feel like giving up?**

2. **When is a time a kid your age might feel afraid and need to ask God for courage?**

3. **What are some ways in which God encourages us?** (He gives us friends and parents and promises of help in the Bible.)

Paper Challenge
Encouraging others can help them trust in God too.

Materials
- Bible with a bookmark at 1 Thessalonians 5:14
- 1 or more of these materials: toilet paper, crepe-paper strip, yarn, curling ribbon, narrow fabric strip

Introduction
God tells us in His Word that He wants us to help people who are weak. Watch to see what is weak in this experiment and what makes the weak item become strong.

Presentation

1. Invite a volunteer to come forward. Ask the volunteer to hold wrists together in front of him- or herself as you wrap one strand of toilet paper around the wrists. Challenge the volunteer to break free.

2. Repeat several times, each time adding one or two strands of paper before the volunteer tries to break free. **One or two strands of paper are weak and we can break them easily. The more strands of paper we add, the stronger the paper becomes.** Repeat with other volunteers and/or materials.

Conclusion
When we try to trust in God by ourselves, we might seem as weak as one strand of paper. We might find it hard to do what God says. But when others help us and encourage us, it's easier to trust God. We are stronger together—just as the papers were stronger when they were put together. **Count the ways this verse says we can help others.** Read 1 Thessalonians 5:14 aloud. Pray, asking God to show children ways of helping others to trust Him.

Discussion Questions

1. **When might it be hard for a kid to do what God wants? How could a friend help that kid to obey?** (pray for that kid, say helpful words)

2. **What's something you know God wants you to do?** (be honest, stand up for someone who needs help) **How could you also help a friend obey God in that way?**

3. **Who has helped you learn about God and trust in Him?**

Faithfulness

A Faithful Watchman

God showed His faithfulness in keeping His promise to send the Savior.

Materials
- Bible with a bookmark at Psalm 117
- items security guards use (flashlight, keys, walkie talkie, handcuffs, etc.)

Introduction
God showed His faithfulness when He kept His promise to send Jesus to be our Savior. Let's find out about someone who trusted God's faithfulness and was faithful to God.

Presentation

1. Show the items you brought. **Watchmen, or security guards, use things like these to help them protect buildings and people and make sure that they are safe. Just like watchmen watch for problems and tell people what they need to know to be safe, preachers pray for people and tell them what they need to know to become members of God's family and be saved from sin's punishment.**

2. **In the early 1920s, a man in China changed his name from Nee Shu-tsu** (sometimes spelled differently) **to Watchman Nee. He chose this name because while his mother had prayed for him to be born, she listened to the night watchman make his rounds. When Nee Shu-tsu heard that his mother promised God her son would love and obey Him, Nee Shu-tsu decided the name Watchman would remind him and others of his plan to serve God. For the rest of his life, Watchman Nee did his best to be faithful in obeying God. One day Watchman received a letter asking him to preach in the city of Chien-O. He wanted to go, but the boat trip to Chien-O cost $80 and Watchman only had $10. Watchman asked for God's help and then went to the river. There was a small boat going to Chien-O for only $7! Watchman Nee's faithful dependence on God meant that others could hear about God.**

Conclusion

Read Psalm 117:1–2 aloud. **What do these verses tell us about God? How did Watchman Nee show he was faithful to God?** (He obeyed God, even when he didn't know how God would provide for him.) Lead the children in prayer, thanking God for His faithfulness.

Discussion Questions

1. **How has God shown faithfulness to us?** (He kept His promise to send Jesus. He makes us part of His family when we trust in Him. He keeps His promises to love and be with us.) Talk with interested children about becoming members of God's family (see "Leading a Child to Christ" on p. 8).

2. **When might people today have a hard time trusting God's faithfulness? What could you say or do to encourage someone in a situation like this?**

3. **How does knowing about God's faithfulness help us?** (We can depend on Him.)

Additional Information for Older Children

During the same year he became a Christian, Watchman Nee began writing books and articles for newspapers. Many Christians still read and learn from Watchman Nee's books. In 1952 Watchman Nee was arrested and put in prison because of his belief in God. He died in prison on March 30, 1972.

Escape from Germany
Acting in ways that demonstrate belief in God shows faithfulness.

Materials
- Bible with a bookmark at Proverbs 20:11
- star cut from yellow construction paper or fabric

Introduction
When we're faithful to God, it means that our actions and words show obedience to God. Let's find out how one person showed his faithfulness to God in a very difficult and scary time.

Presentation

1. Show the yellow star. **When people called Nazis were in control of Germany during World War II, Jewish people were forced to wear stars like this on their clothes. The Nazis wanted everyone to hate Jewish people. Not all the German people agreed with the Nazis. A German man named Dietrich (DEE-trihk) Bonhoeffer (BAHN-hahf-uhr) dared to help people who wore yellow stars.**

2. **Dietrich Bonhoeffer was a pastor in Germany during World War II. Many other German pastors would not help Jewish people, because they were afraid of Hitler and the Nazi army, but Dietrich said this was not right! Dietrich did more than just say it was wrong to hate Jewish people; he did what he could to help them. One time Dietrich helped a group of Jewish people escape from Germany. He had papers that gave him permission to travel in and out of Germany. On one trip, he took some Jews with him. German guards stopped the car, but because of his permission papers, the guards let him leave Germany—along with the Jewish people in his car. Later, the Nazis found out what he was doing and arrested him. While he was in prison, Dietrich wrote several books about faithfully serving God. Dietrich was eventually killed because of his actions that showed his belief in God. People today still read the books he wrote and remember how important it is to be faithful to do what is right.**

Conclusion
Read Proverbs 20:11 aloud. **What are some actions that showed Pastor Bonhoeffer's belief in God? How did this pastor's actions make a difference?** Lead children in prayer, asking God to help them be faithful in showing belief in God.

Discussion Questions

1. **How do kids your age show they believe in God?** (They don't go along with the crowd in doing wrong; they go to church, read their Bibles, pray and ask God for help when they have problems, and treat others kindly.)

2. **How do you think your faithfulness to God might help another person?**

3. **When are some times you have seen other people show their belief in God?** Briefly share your own answer before you ask for responses.

4. **How can you show faithfulness to God when you are with your friends? When you are with your family?**

Additional Information for Older Children

While in prison, Dietrich wrote many letters. His letters to the woman he was planning to marry were collected into a book called *Love Letters from Cell 92*. On the day Dietrich was killed, the prison doctor saw him praying in his cell. The doctor later said that in all his years as a doctor, he had never seen anyone more faithful about doing God's will.

Faith of a Mother

The habits we form by being faithful to God help us do what is right, even when trouble comes.

Materials
- Bible with a bookmark at Proverbs 3:3
- clock with hour and minute hands
- bookmarks, hymnals *(optional)*

Introduction
The habits we form by being faithful to God help us do what is right at all times. Let's look at some different things we can do with our time.

Presentation

1. Show the clock. **How long does it take for the short hand to move from one number to another?** Let children respond. **What are some things you can do in an hour?** (watch [two] cartoon shows, drive to [a location approximately 60 miles away], attend soccer practice)

2. **One person who lived a long time ago had a habit of doing something for two hours every day. Susanna Wesley, a woman who lived in England in the 1700s, prayed for two hours every day. Even though Susanna had many children to take care of and was very busy with all kinds of work, every day she stopped whatever she was doing to pray and think about God's Word for one hour in the morning and one hour in the evening. Susanna began this habit of showing love and obedience to God when her children were young, and she faithfully continued the habit throughout her life. She had two sons who became famous preachers and songwriters—God used them to tell the good news of Jesus all over England!**

Conclusion
Read Proverbs 3:3 aloud. **What are some habits Proverbs 3:3 talks about?** (showing love and being faithful to God) **How did Susanna Wesley obey this verse?** (She prayed and thought about God's Word every day.) **What are some other habits that show love and faithfulness to God?** Lead children in prayer, thanking God for His love and asking for His help in showing love and faithfulness to Him.

Discussion Questions

1. **When you "bind something around your neck" or "write it on the tablet of your heart" (know it by heart), it means you are trying to keep that thing close to you so that you will never lose it. What is Proverbs 3:3 telling us not to lose?** (love and faithfulness to God)

2. **What does it mean to be faithful to God?** (to love Him with all your heart, soul, mind, and strength and to obey God's commands no matter what)

3. **What kinds of habits could you form that would show your faithfulness to God?** (reading the Bible to learn more about God, praying to God every day, obeying God's commands)

4. **How can these habits help you when things are hard?** (Knowing God's Word will help a person know the right thing to do, even in difficult situations. Praying to God will be comforting in times of fear or sadness.)

Additional Information for Older Children

One of Susanna Wesley's sons, Charles Wesley, wrote many songs called hymns that are still sung in churches today. *(Optional: Use bookmarks to mark several of Charles Wesley's hymns in some church hymnals: "Love Divine, All Loves Excelling," "Hark! The Herald Angels Sing," "Jesus, Lover of My Soul," "O for a Thousand Tongues to Sing," "Christ the Lord Is Risen Today," etc. Children can find and read some of the songs.* **Can you find words or phrases that remind you of showing love? Of being faithful?**)

Faithful Friendship
Faithfulness to others means being a friend in good and bad times.

Materials
- Bible with a bookmark at Proverbs 17:17
- sleeping bag or pillow
- large sheet of paper or whiteboard, marker *(optional)*

Introduction
Showing faithfulness means being a good friend no matter what—in good and bad times. Let's find out how one man showed he was a faithful friend.

Presentation
1. Show the sleeping bag or pillow. **When do you use this?** (camping, sleeping overnight at a friend's house) **One way to show friendship is to stay overnight at a friend's house. One man showed friendship by doing more than staying overnight with his friends. This man chose to live with the people that he wanted to be friends with.**

2. **David Zeisberger lived in the 1800s. During that time many Native Americans were being cheated out of the land they lived on. White people and Native Americans weren't usually friends. But David was a missionary who wanted to tell the good news about Jesus to a Native American tribe called the Iroquois (IHR-eh-kwoi). So David went to live with the Iroquois and learned to speak their language. He didn't try to make the people change the ways they dressed or ate. And instead of cheating the Iroquois out of their land, David helped them build towns of their own. David was a faithful friend. Later when the members of David's church wanted to become missionaries to the Iroquois, the tribe didn't want these missionaries to come. White people had cheated them too many times! But one of the Iroquois called David a friend and a brother. Others who knew David agreed that David had proven to be a fair and faithful friend to the Iroquois people. He had even gone to jail instead of giving up his friendship with them. Because of David's friendship, the Iroquois allowed the missionaries to tell them about Jesus.**

Conclusion

Read Proverbs 17:17 aloud. **Someone who is faithful shows friendship in good and bad times. How did David Zeisberger show faithfulness to his friends?** (He learned their language. He helped them build towns.) **Let's thank God for being faithful to us and loving us at all times.** Lead children in prayer. Talk with interested children about becoming members of God's family (see "Leading a Child to Christ" on p. 8).

Discussion Questions

1. **Who has been a faithful friend to you? What has this person done to show friendship to you?**

2. **When is it hard to show friendship to others?**

3. **How can you be a good friend to someone who has a hard time learning at school or to someone who has a hard time getting along with others?**

4. **Why might kids your age have a hard time continuing to be a faithful friend to someone?** (when that person moves away, when the person stops being nice, when we find new friends) **What can we do to remember to be faithful friends, even when it's hard?** (We can ask God's help and remember the words of Proverbs 17:17.)

Additional Information for Older Children

David Zeisberger was such a good friend to the Native Americans that one tribe even adopted him into their tribe. This tribe called David Zeisberger their brother and gave him a Native-American name. *(Optional: Print the name of the tribe, "Onandag," and the name they gave David Zeisberger, "Ganousaracherie," on a large sheet of paper or whiteboard. Show the paper to the children.)* **Because David was adopted into this tribe, many other tribes also welcomed him as their friend.**

Helicopter Project

When we show love for God by working together, good things can be accomplished.

Materials
- Bible with a bookmark at Colossians 3:23
- 4 strips of paper ³/₄" x 6"
- scissors
- ruler
- paper clips
- additional materials as indicated *(optional)*

Introduction
Whenever there is a big or small project to be done, it helps to have more than one good worker. God wants us to do good work to show our love for Him. Today we'll work together to make paper helicopters. Each of you will have a part to do.

Presentation

1. Select four volunteers. Volunteers should stand in a single-file line at a table. Give the first volunteer the four paper strips, scissors, and ruler. Hand the third volunteer the paper clips.

2. The first volunteer cuts a 2" slit in the top of each paper strip (see sketch a). The second volunteer folds the lower corners of each strip to a point (see sketch b). The third volunteer attaches a paper clip to the folded part of the strip (see sketch c). The fourth volunteer folds one half of the cut portion of the strips in one direction and the other half in the opposite direction (see sketch d).

3. Volunteers fly the helicopters by holding the paper clip and tossing the helicopters up in the air.

Conclusion

Because each person did his or her part, we were able to make helicopters. **Why does Colossians 3:23 say it's important to do our best work?** Read the verse aloud. **A good way to show love for God is by working together with other people.** Ask God's help in working with others to do the good things God wants us to do.

Discussion Questions

1. **What might have happened if someone didn't do careful work in making the helicopter?**

2. **What are some times kids need to do their best job when working with others to complete a project?** (school projects, sports teams)

3. **What are some examples of ways in which people who live together need to work together?** (cleaning up after dinner, decorating a Christmas tree, picking up leaves)

4. **What's one way you can help someone else by doing your best work?**

Job Training
Show faithfulness by doing what God wants you to do.

Materials
- Bible with a bookmark at Galatians 6:9
- tablecloth
- place setting (plate, utensils, glass)

Introduction
When we do what God wants us to, we show faithfulness to God. Let's find out about a woman who helped others learn to show faithfulness.

Presentation

1. Invite volunteers to use the items you brought to show how to set a table. **For what kinds of jobs would you need to know how to set a table?** (waiter) **What are some other jobs you know of?** Volunteers can answer. **In the early 1900s many African Americans had a hard time finding good jobs. Mary McLeod Bethune was an African American schoolteacher who wanted her students to be able to get good jobs.**

2. **Mary started a school for African American children. She taught her students how to read, how to study Bible stories, and how to speak a language called Latin. She also taught practical skills like setting tables, cooking, gardening, sewing, and cleaning. Mary wanted her students to have a good education, and she wanted them to have practical skills so that they could get good jobs. One day some of the students had to wash white linen tablecloths. Mary told the girls to boil the tablecloths to get the tablecloths clean. But the girls didn't want to make a fire and wait for the water in the large kettle to boil before they could finish the job! Not much later, Mary saw the girls hanging up the tablecloths to dry. When Mary asked if the girls had boiled the tablecloths, they admitted that they had not. Mary insisted that the girls do the job again—the right way. Mary wanted her students to understand that being faithful and not giving up was important in every job they did, even washing tablecloths.**

Conclusion

Read Galatians 6:9 aloud. **When might kids today show faithfulness?** (caring for a younger brother or sister, doing a chore without being reminded) **What is an example of a way Mary McLeod Bethune taught her students to show faithfulness?** (She made them boil the tablecloths in order to do a good job.) **Let's ask God to help us show faithfulness by doing what He wants.** Lead the children in prayer.

Discussion Questions

1. **What does it mean to be faithful?** (to try to do what God wants all the time)

2. **What are some things that God wants us to do faithfully?** (be fair, tell the truth)

3. **When might kids your age get tired, or grow weary, of obeying God?** (See Galatians 6:9.)

Additional Information for Older Children

Mary McLeod Bethune not only taught others to show faithfulness, but she also showed faithfulness to God herself! Mary attended Moody Bible Institute in Chicago and hoped to become a missionary to Africa. When she wasn't able to do that, she decided to stay in the United States and start a school for African American children. The small school she started with five students in 1904 is now Bethune-Cookman University in Daytona Beach, Florida. Because of Mary's faithfulness, thousands of students still learn about God each year!

Praise the Lord

God gives us abilities and wants us to be faithful in using them.

Whatever you do, work at it with all your heart, as working for the Lord, not for human masters.

Colossians 3:23

Materials
- Bible with a bookmark at Colossians 3:23
- marker
- paper
- suggested books *(optional)*

Introduction
God gives each of us abilities we can be faithful to use. Let's listen to find out how one woman worked hard and was faithful to use her abilities, even when it was hard.

Presentation

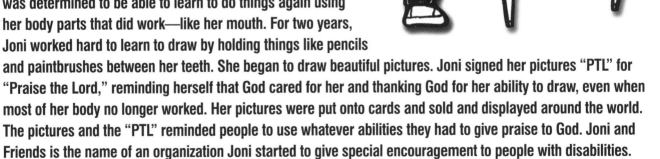

1. Ask a volunteer to put the marker in his or her mouth and try to draw a picture of a tree. **It's pretty hard to draw this way, but this is how a woman named Joni** (JAHN-ee) **Eareckson Tada learned to draw all her pictures!**

2. **Joni didn't always draw this way. When Joni was a teenager, she had an accident. She dove into a lake at a place where the water was too shallow, and she broke her neck and became paralyzed. Joni could no longer use her arms or legs. But Joni was determined to be able to learn to do things again using her body parts that did work—like her mouth. For two years, Joni worked hard to learn to draw by holding things like pencils and paintbrushes between her teeth. She began to draw beautiful pictures. Joni signed her pictures "PTL" for "Praise the Lord," reminding herself that God cared for her and thanking God for her ability to draw, even when most of her body no longer worked. Her pictures were put onto cards and sold and displayed around the world. The pictures and the "PTL" reminded people to use whatever abilities they had to give praise to God. Joni and Friends is the name of an organization Joni started to give special encouragement to people with disabilities.**

Conclusion
Read Colossians 3:23 aloud. **When we are "working for the Lord," it means we are trying to do our best work to show love for God. What did Joni Eareckson Tada do to obey this verse? How did she show that she was working to please God?** (She signed her pictures "Praise the Lord.") Lead the children in prayer, thanking God for the abilities He has given us.

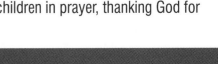

Discussion Questions

1. **What does it mean to be faithful?** (to keep doing something you said you would do, to keep your promises)

2. **What are some of the things you like to do or are good at doing?** Encourage children to think beyond obvious talents, such as reading well or playing sports, to abilities, such as being a good friend or listening well.

3. **What are some ways to be faithful in using the abilities God has given you?** (practice using the abilities, keep using them to help others, have a good attitude while using the abilities)

4. **How can you use those abilities to serve God or help others?** Answer this question with an example from your own life before asking children to respond.

Additional Information for Older Children

People were so amazed at Joni's story they encouraged her to write a book about her life. Joni wrote an autobiography, and a movie was also made about her life. Now Joni has used her abilities to illustrate and write more books. (*Optional: Bring a copy of her autobiography,* Joni, *to lend to an older child, or bring any of Joni's children's books*—Tell Me the Truth, Tell Me the Promises, You've Got a Friend—*for children to borrow and read.*)

Who's First?

We show our faithfulness to God by making good choices.

Materials
- Bible with a bookmark at Psalm 119:30
- coin
- 2 straws or paper strips of different lengths
- baseball bat or stick

Introduction
Every day we make many choices—like what we're going to wear and what we're going to eat. Some choices, however, are more important than others and show our faithfulness to God. Let's talk about some of the ways we make choices.

Presentation
1. **How do you and your friends choose who will take the first turn in a game?** Volunteers can answer.

2. Lead volunteers to take turns participating in one or more of these ways of choosing: (A) Toss a coin in the air. Two volunteers call heads or tails. (B) Hold straws or paper strips with the lower end hidden so that they appear to be the same length. Two volunteers choose straws or paper strips to see which is the longest. (C) Beginning at one end of a bat or stick, two volunteers alternate grasping hold of the bat to see whose hand is the last hand placed at the other end of the bat. (D) Choose a number between 1 and 20. Two or more volunteers guess the number. (E) Place your hands behind your back holding a coin in one hand. Two volunteers choose which hand they think holds the coin.

Conclusion
These kinds of choices help us when we're playing games. But the Bible talks about the most important choice of all: whether or not we will be faithful to God. **What does Psalm 119:30 say about this important choice?** Read the verse aloud. **Choosing the way of faithfulness means to choose to believe in and obey God. When. we make good choices, we show that we want to love and obey God.** Ask God for help in making good choices.

Discussion Questions

1. **Who is someone you think makes good choices? Why?**

2. **What are some good choices kids your age can make at school? At home? How do these choices show love and obedience to God?**

3. **What might make it hard to make a good choice?** (when you want to do something else, when others might make fun of you) **Who does God provide to help you make good choices and show faithfulness to God?** (family, friends, the Holy Spirit)

Forgiveness

"Awe"some Forgiveness

God's forgiveness of our sins helps us forgive others, even when they don't deserve it.

Materials
- Bible with bookmarks at Psalm 139:23–24 and Ephesians 4:32
- large sheet of paper or whiteboard
- marker

> **Be kind and compassionate to one another, forgiving each other, just as in Christ God forgave you.**
>
> Ephesians 4:32

Preparation
Print several misspelled words and incorrect math problems on a large sheet of paper or whiteboard, adjusting the difficulty of teh spelling and math according to the age of your children.

Introduction
Because God forgives us when we ask, we can forgive others, even when they don't ask! In Old Testament times, there were ten days during which God especially wanted His people to carefully think about the sins for which they needed to be forgiven. Let's find out about these ten days and what it means to carefully look for something wrong.

Presentation

1. **The ten days between the Feast (or Festival) of Trumpets and the Day of Atonement are now called the Days of Awe by modern-day Jewish people. What do you think of when you hear the word *awe*?** (awesome, things that are very good or beautiful) **The word *awe* means those things, but it also means "respect, admiration, and amazement." During the "Days of Awe" in Bible times, as God's people thought about how wonderful and perfect God is, they also thought about their own lives and realized the wrong things they had said and done.**

2. Show the paper you prepared. Invite volunteers to correct the spelling and math. **In order to find what was wrong with these words and problems, we looked carefully for what was wrong. In the same way, during the Days of Awe, people examined their actions so they knew what sins to ask forgiveness for.**

3. **When we believe in Jesus and become members of God's family, we are forgiven once and for all—forever. But the Bible says we should still look carefully at our lives and make sure they are pleasing to God.** Read or ask a child to read Psalm 139:23–24.

Conclusion

Knowing we are forgiven should make us want to please God more and more. Being forgiven makes us want to do something else. Read Ephesians 4:32 aloud. **What does God's forgiveness help us want to do?** (forgive others) Pray, thanking God that when we ask, He forgives our sins and helps us want to forgive others.

Discussion Questions

1. **When can kids your age forgive others?** (when others cheat you or lie to you)

2. **What can we do to show forgiveness?** (say "I forgive you," smile, be friendly)

3. **Why does God's forgiveness help us forgive others, even if they don't deserve it?** (God forgives us, even when we don't deserve it. To show our thankfulness to God, we show His love to others by forgiving them.)

Additional Information for Older Children

Invite several older children to take turns reading these verses that describe God's forgiveness and love: Psalm 103:1–4, 8–13.

A Sweet New Year

God's forgiveness is for everyone who believes in Jesus.

Materials
- Bible with a bookmark at Acts 10:43
- apples
- knife
- bowls
- lemon juice
- honey
- napkins

Preparation
Slice the apples and place them in bowls. Drizzle the apple slices with lemon juice to prevent browning. Pour approximately $1/3$ cup of honey into different bowls. Prepare one bowl of slices and one bowl of honey for every six to eight children.

Introduction
No matter how old or young we are or how many good or bad things we've done, we can receive God's forgiveness when we believe in Jesus. Since long ago, the Jewish people (called Hebrews in Bible times) have celebrated a holiday that reminds them of their need or forgiveness. This holiday is called the Feast (or Festival) of Trumpets.

Presentation
1. **The Feast of Trumpets got its name because it began with the sounds of a trumpet called a shofar** (SHOH-fahr). *(Optional: Older children can read Leviticus 23:23–24.)* **This holiday was the beginning of a time of year when God wanted His people to turn away from their sins—the wrong things they had done. This was a time to realize they needed God's forgiveness for their wrong actions.**

2. **Rosh Hashanah** (RAHSH huh-SHAH-nuh) **is another name for this celebration; it means "new year." The Hebrew calendar started a new year in the fall. Rosh Hashanah reminds people to start the new year by celebrating God's loving forgiveness. To celebrate the new year, special foods are eaten. What are some special foods you eat at parties or celebrations?** (birthday cake, Thanksgiving turkey) **Apples dipped in honey are eaten at Rosh Hashanah to show that a sweet or good new year is hoped for.** Let children dip the apple slices into honey before eating.

Conclusion

Apples and honey remind us that God gives us many good things. God's greatest gift is that when people believe in Jesus and admit their sin, God forgives them. Read Acts 10:43 aloud. Thank God for His forgiveness. Talk with interested children about becoming members of God's family (see "Leading a Child to Christ" on p. 8).

Discussion Questions

1. What are some things people might think they have to do to be forgiven? (go to church, read their Bibles) Those are all good things to do, but who does Acts 10:43 say can have their sins forgiven? (Anyone who asks God for forgiveness of sin and who believes in Jesus.)

2. What does it mean to believe in Jesus? (to believe Jesus is God's Son and He died to take the punishment for our sins)

3. How can we be sure our sins are forgiven? (God always keeps His promises.)

Additional Information for Older Children

In the Old Testament book of Micah, we can read about God's forgiveness of sin. Ask a volunteer to read Micah 7:18–19. How do these verses describe God's forgiveness of sin? As a reminder that God takes away all sin, on Rosh Hashanah Jewish people throw bread crumbs into the ocean or a river and watch the crumbs disappear.

Debt Free

When we realize how much we have been forgiven, we become more willing to forgive others.

Materials
- Bible with a bookmark at Luke 6:37
- a variety of household bills

Introduction
Because God has forgiven us, we are to forgive others too! In Bible times, God's people celebrated a holiday that reminds us how important it is to forgive others. This holiday, called the Year of Jubilee, was celebrated once every 50 years! Let's find out what happened in this holiday.

Presentation

1. Show children the bills you brought and make a comment such as, **When I get bills like these, it means I have to pay someone for the gasoline I've put in my car and for the electricity and water I've used in my house. Until I've paid these bills, I'm in debt, which means I owe money. How do you think I would feel if someone told me I didn't have to pay these bills?** (excited, happy, glad)

2. **During the Year of Jubilee if you owed someone money, your debt was taken away, or forgiven. Slaves were set free! And if you had sold land to someone, that land would be returned to you. God wanted His people to celebrate the Year of Jubilee so poor people would receive the help they needed. The word** *jubilee* **means "liberty" or "freedom." This holiday was celebrated the whole year long!** *(Optional: Older children can read Leviticus 25:10; 27:24.)*

Conclusion
God thinks forgiving others is so important that He doesn't want us to do it only once every 50 years. Read Luke 6:37 aloud. **The Bible teaches us that because God has forgiven us, He wants us to forgive others every day.** Pray, thanking God for His forgiveness and asking His help in forgiving others.

Discussion Questions

1. **In what ways do people today show that they forgive others?** (treat the person kindly, be friendly, say "I forgive you")

2. **When has someone forgiven you? How did you know you were forgiven?**

Additional Information for Older Children

Jesus made it very clear that He places a high priority on forgiveness of others. Read Jesus' story of a forgiving king in Matthew 18:21–35.

Fast and Slow
God is eager to love and forgive us.

Materials
- Bible with a bookmark at Psalm 145:8
- scrap paper
- pencil
- coin
- crackers
- timer *(optional)*

> **The LORD is gracious and compassionate, slow to anger and rich in love.**
> Psalm 145:8

Introduction
God's love and forgiveness are so amazing that the Bible talks about them in many different ways. Let's do some actions that help us understand the ways in which God treats us.

Presentation
1. Invite volunteers to take turns seeing how slowly and then how quickly they can complete a variety of tasks: do three jumping jacks, write their names, crumple up four pieces of paper, flip a coin five times, eat a cracker. Select different volunteers for each fast and slow action. *(Optional: Time the children, limiting the slow actions to about 30 seconds.)* If time is short, ask more than one volunteer to complete the tasks at the same time.

2. **Your actions were good examples of what it means to do things slowly and what it means to do things quickly. Psalm 145:8 tells us something God is slow to do and something God is quick to do.** Read the verse aloud. **What does this verse say God is slow to do?** (be angry) **What does this verse say God is eager to give us a lot of?** (His love) **God cares for each of us so much that He is eager and glad to show His love to us. He is quick to forgive us when we've done wrong things.**

Conclusion
Lead the children in prayer, thanking God for His love and forgiveness.

Discussion Questions

1. **What stories about Bible people help you want to love and obey God?**

2. **How can kids your age show faith in God?** (do what God says in the Bible, pray to God and ask His help in loving Him and others)

3. **Who is someone you know who loves and obeys God? What can you learn about how to obey God from that person's example?** (learn to tell the truth, learn to be patient)

4. **What are some ways kids your age can be examples of ways to love and obey God?**

Have a Seat!
God's patience and forgiveness show us how to be patient with others.

Materials
- Bible with a bookmark at 1 Corinthians 13:7
- newspaper

Introduction
God shows patience by forgiving us and loving us, even when we don't deserve it. When we realize God's patience with us, it helps us be patient with others. Let's find out how some people showed patience.

Presentation

1. Give each child a sheet of newspaper. **What can you do with a newspaper?** Children can demonstrate their ideas. **In China, some people used newspapers in an unusual way.**

2. **Pastor Li was the leader of a church in China that met in a house. It was against the law for this church to meet and for Pastor Li to preach about Jesus. But he didn't stop. Because of his preaching, Pastor Li was arrested and severely beaten many times. One day the police came to the church meeting and not only took every Bible they found, but they also took all the chairs! Still, the people didn't give up meeting together. They patiently folded up newspapers to sit on instead of chairs and kept right on meeting together and worshipping God.** *(Optional: Let children fold the newspapers, place them on the floor, and sit on them.)* **The people even prayed for the police and thanked God for the opportunity to talk about Jesus.**

Conclusion
Read 1 Corinthians 13:7 aloud. **What word in this verse means the same thing as patient?** (perseveres) **To persevere means to keep on doing something, even when it's hard. When we remember God's patience toward us, it helps us keep on showing patience to others. How did Pastor Li and the people in his church show patience?** (They kept worshipping God and praying for others, even when the police made it hard.) Pray, thanking God for His patience and asking His help in showing patience toward others.

Discussion Questions

1. **How does God show patience toward us?** (He forgives us when we're sorry. He takes care of us even when we don't thank Him.)

2. **When is a time you need to keep on showing patience toward others?** (when others make fun of me, when others don't keep their promises)

3. **What are some ways you could show patience with others?** (not yelling back when someone starts yelling, waiting to take a turn without complaining, praying every day for a friend who is sick even if he or she doesn't get well right away)

4. **What can help you show patience when it's hard?** (remembering God's love for me)

Additional Information for Older Children

One night as Pastor Li was preaching, the police came and arrested him. Instead of fighting with them, Pastor Li and his people simply prayed for the police. As the police took Pastor Li to their car, they noticed he was carrying a bag with him. They asked him what was in the bag. Pastor Li explained that the bag had a blanket and some clothes in it. Three years earlier, the police had threatened to arrest him, so Pastor Li had packed a bag that he kept for three years in case the police came back to arrest him.

Laundry Day

God's great love in sending Jesus to die for our sins is shown to others when we forgive them.

Materials
- Bible with a bookmark at Colossians 3:13
- laundry basket and/or detergent

Bear with each other and forgive one another if any of you has a grievance against someone. Forgive as the Lord forgave you.

Colossians 3:13

Introduction
When we have been forgiven by God, we can show His love to other people by forgiving them. Let's find out how a woman helped some people forgive each other and show God's love.

Presentation

1. Show the laundry basket and/or detergent. **What are these things used for?** Allow children to respond. Before washing machines had been invented, it took people many hours to wash and iron their clothes. People often hired others to do their laundry.

2. Amanda Smith was a former slave who earned money by doing laundry for others. After her husband died, she had to work hard to earn enough money to care for her family. Amanda also worked hard so she could have enough money to travel and spend time telling others about God's love and forgiveness. One day after hearing Amanda speak, a young man asked for help. The man had fought with a friend several years before. Amanda's teaching helped the young man see that he needed to forgive his friend, but he was afraid to speak to him. Amanda prayed for the young man and said God would help him. The next day, the young man saw the man he had fought with. Even though he was afraid, the young man walked up to him and started to speak. The other man said, "I'm so glad you came to talk to me. I wanted to say something, but I was afraid you wouldn't speak to me!" The two men quickly forgave each other and became good friends again. Amanda felt that seeing those two men forgive each other was worth all the clothes she had to wash in order to have time to tell others about God and His love.

Conclusion

Read Colossians 3:13 aloud. **How did Amanda Smith help the two friends obey this verse?** Let children respond. **Let's thank God for forgiving us and ask God to help us have courage to obey this verse and forgive others.** Lead children in prayer.

Discussion Questions

1. When have you needed to forgive a friend? What happened when you forgave your friend?

2. Why is forgiveness important? What do you think might happen to friendships if neither friend is willing to forgive the other one?

3. How does forgiveness help people get along with each other better?

Additional Information for Older Children

Amanda Smith was a friend to people all over the world! She traveled to countries all over the world to tell others about Jesus. She also started a home and school for orphaned African American girls in Harvey, Illinois. Amanda also wrote her autobiography, which tells about her faith in God and her missionary travels in America, England, Ireland, Scotland, India, and Africa.

Road Signs

Admit when you've done wrong, and ask God's help to change your actions.

I have considered my ways and have turned my steps to your statutes.

Psalm 119:59

Materials
- Bible with a bookmark at Psalm 119:59
- separate sheets of paper on which you have drawn road signs (see sketches)

Introduction
God wants us to think carefully about His commands and how we can obey them. Let's talk about what we can do when we have disobeyed God.

Presentation

1. One at a time, show each of the road signs you drew. **What would the driver of a car need to do to obey this sign?** Let volunteers answer. Explain the road signs as needed.

2. **Which of these signs help us know what to do when we realize we have disobeyed God?** Children can offer ideas. **The stop sign reminds us that we should stop doing what's wrong. The U-turn sign tells us we should turn away from doing wrong and start doing what God says is right.**

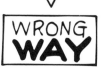

Conclusion
Read Psalm 119:59 aloud. **What word in this verse means the same as commands?** (statutes) **Psalm 119:59 reminds us to choose to obey God's commands. None of us is perfect; but when we disobey God, we can tell God we're sorry and ask His help in making a U-turn—turning away from our wrong actions and doing what's right.** Pray, asking God for help in obeying Him and thanking Him for forgiving us when we sin.

Discussion Questions

1. What other signs have you seen on the road?

2. What's an example of a time a kid your age might choose to stop doing something wrong and start doing something right?

3. When are times you are tempted to disobey God?

4. Who can help you obey God instead of disobeying Him? (God promises to help us obey. God gives us parents, teachers, and friends to help us obey.)

Shofar Sounds
God's forgiveness helps us make a new start.

Materials
- Bible with a bookmark at 2 Corinthians 5:17
- shofar (or trumpet or other horn or recorded horn sounds and music player), rhythm instruments (optional)

> **If anyone is in Christ, the new creation has come: The old has gone, the new is here!**
>
> 2 Corinthians 5:17

Introduction
When we believe in Jesus, God's forgiveness helps us make a brand-new start. God forgives the wrong things we have done. In the Old Testament, the sound of a trumpet reminded the people of their need for forgiveness. Let's find out what happened.

Presentation
1. (Optional: Play blasts of a shofar or other horn.) **When do you hear trumpets or other horns blow?** (parades, concerts, church) **In Bible times, God's people played trumpets as signals. On the holiday called Feast (or Festival) of Trumpets, the sound of a trumpet called a shofar signaled the people to remember their need for God's forgiveness. Shofars were made from the horns of rams.**

2. **At the Feast of Trumpets, also called Rosh Hashanah** (RAHSH huh-SHAH-nuh)**, the shofar is played in a special way.** Clap your hands in this pattern: one clap followed by a long pause, three claps, nine fast and short claps, one clap. Invite children to clap hands in this same pattern, repeating the pattern several times. (Optional: Blow the pattern on a shofar or any single note of trumpet or horn or play recorded sounds. Children can play the pattern with rhythm instruments.)

Conclusion
In Bible times at the Feast of Trumpets, God's people would think about the wrong things they had done. When we think about our sins, we can ask God to forgive us, and He will! Jesus' death on the cross makes it possible for our sins to be forgiven. Read 2 Corinthians 5:17 aloud. Lead children in prayer, thanking God for forgiving our sins.

Discussion Questions

1. **According to 2 Corinthians 5:17, "The old has gone, the new is here!" What does this mean?** (When you become a member of God's family, you don't have to feel guilty for the wrong things you have done. You have a new chance to obey God and do right things without worrying about the past.)

2. **When are some times kids your age need to ask forgiveness?**

3. **How do we know God forgives us?** (He sent Jesus to take the punishment for our sin. God promises to forgive us when we are sorry for what we have done and ask for His forgiveness.)

Additional Information for Older Children

The sound of the trumpets not only signaled a time for the people to get ready for the forgiveness of their sins but also signaled a new year was beginning. (In Bible times, the people didn't have calendars to keep track of what day of the week or year it was. They followed the cycles of the moon.) The words *Rosh Hashanah* actually mean "new year." **When do we celebrate the beginning of the new year?** (New Year's Eve in the month of December) **Lets find out the season of the year in which the Hebrew people in Bible times celebrated their new year.** A volunteer can read Leviticus 23:23–25 to find the information: the Hebrew people's seventh month which is the fall of our year—the months of September or October.

God's Word

Action Words

God's words are valuable because they show us the best ways to live.

> **I love your commands more than gold, more than pure gold.**
>
> Psalm 119:127

Materials
Bible with a bookmark Psalm 119:127

Introduction
The words we say can't be seen, but they can be powerful. Let's talk about why words—especially God's words—can be so powerful.

Presentation

1. Whisper "Fire!" to a volunteer who then acts out a response to the word. Other children in the group try to identify the word. Give clues as needed to help children guess. After the word is guessed ask, **Why is the word fire powerful?** (It gives us important information. Knowing about a fire can save our lives.)

2. Repeat the activity with other volunteers and these words or phrases: *stop*, *free candy*, *home run*, *goal*, *I'm not it*, *dinner's ready*, *on your mark—get set—go*, *foul ball*.

Conclusion
Why do you think God's words or commands are so powerful? (They help us know the best way to live. They tell us how to obey God instead of sinning.) **Because God's commands help us in so many ways, the Bible says they are very valuable.** Read Psalm 119:127 aloud. **If this verse were written today, what words might be substituted for the word *gold*?** Pray, thanking God for His commands and asking His help to obey them.

Discussion Questions

1. **What are some other powerful things that can't be seen?** (wind, thunder)

2. **What are some ways kids your age can show they think God's commands are valuable?**

3. **How has one of God's commands helped you know what to do or say?** Tell children about a time one of God's commands has helped you.

Bibles and Books

God's Word tells us the good news about Jesus and helps us grow in God's family.

Materials

- Bible with a bookmark at Psalm 32:8
- examples of instruction books (computer book, cookbook, appliance manual, textbook, etiquette book, etc.)
- sheet of paper for each child

Introduction

The Bible is a collection of books. It tells us the good news about Jesus and helps us grow in God's family. Let's compare God's Word with other books that help us.

Presentation

1. Display the instruction books one at a time, and ask questions such as, **What kind of book is this? What does it help us do?** Accept responses. **What do all these books have in common?** (They help people learn to do something.)

2. **All of these books help us learn how to do things.** Show the Bible. **What makes this book different from all these other books?** (It's God's messages to us.) **God's Word helps us learn much more important information than how to work a computer or _____** (substitute words specific to the instruction books you brought). **The instructions in God's Word help us know the right way to live so that we can show our love to God and others.**

3. **Let's follow instructions and make something to remind us that God's Word tells us the good news about Jesus and helps us grow in God's family.** Give each child a sheet of paper. Instruct children to fold the paper in half lengthwise. Then tell children to fold the top third down. Children tear out a rectangular shape from the nonfolded edges (see sketch a). When the paper is unfolded, children will have made a torn-paper cross (see sketch b). **When we see a cross, it reminds us of the way in which Jesus died to take the punishment for our sins. Jesus' death and resurrection are the good news the Bible tells us about.**

Conclusion

Read Psalm 32:8 aloud. **What does Psalm 32:8 say God will do for us?** (instruct and teach us about the right way to live) **What are some ways God teaches us?** (through His Word, through parents and teachers) **God's instructions show us how to grow as members of God's family. This is a great reason to celebrate!** Pray, praising God and thanking Him for His help in learning the right way to live.

Discussion Questions

1. **What good news do you learn about Jesus from reading the Bible?** (Jesus died on the cross to pay for our sins. Jesus rose from the dead. Jesus healed and cared for many people.)

2. **How does the Bible help us grow in God's family?** (The Bible tells us how to become a part of God's family: believe Jesus died for our sins and ask for forgiveness. When we read the Bible, we can learn the good things God wants His family members to do.)

3. **When can you read or hear about God's Word?** (at school, playing a game during recess, at home with family)

4. **What are some of the ways the Bible tells us to live?** (love God, love our neighbors, be kind and help others, tell the truth, obey our parents, tell others about God)

Additional Information for Older Children

In some Bibles, two phrases are written under the title of Psalm 32: "Of David" and "A maskil." **What does "of David" mean?** (David wrote the psalm.) **David wrote this psalm as a conversation between himself and God.** Volunteers can read verse 5 as an example of David's words and verse 8 as an example of God's words. *Maskil* **is a Hebrew word that means "any who understand." That means that the psalm was written for anyone who would follow the instructions in it.**

Follow the Light

We can learn the very best way to live from God's Word.

> **Your word is a lamp for my feet, a light on my path.**
> Psalm 119:105

Materials
- Bible with a bookmark at Psalm 119:105
- flashlight or laser penlight
- index card on which you have written the words of Psalm 119:105

Introduction
God's Word helps us learn to live in the very best way. Because God's Word is so important, it is sometimes compared to a light. Let's use this flashlight to find out how light helps us.

Presentation

1. While a volunteer covers his or her eyes, hide the index card nearby. Then have the volunteer uncover his or her eyes.

2. Use the flashlight or laser penlight to slowly trace on the floor a path the volunteer follows, eventually leading the volunteer to the location of the hidden card. Have the volunteer read the verse aloud.

3. Repeat the activity with other volunteers as time permits, inviting children to take turns hiding the card and using the flashlight. If you have a large group, use the flashlight to direct each volunteer's attention around the room, stopping the light on the location where the card is hidden. The volunteer comes forward to find the card and read it aloud.

4. Discuss the activity by asking, **How did the flashlight help you? Where did the flashlight lead you?**

Conclusion
God's Word, the Bible, is like a light because it shows us the path to follow and the very best way to live. The things we learn in the Bible help us know how to love and obey God. Read Psalm 119:105 aloud. Lead the children in prayer, thanking God for His Word.

Discussion Questions

1. **When might you need a flashlight or other kind of light to help you find your way?**

2. **When do kids your age need help to know how to love and obey God?** (when someone wants to start an argument, when someone is being unkind) **How can God's Word help us in those situations?** (helps us know what to say and do, gives us commands to follow)

God's Word in English
Patiently keep doing what God wants you to do.

Materials
- Bible with a bookmark at 1 Kings 8:61
- several different versions of the Bible and/or several written in different languages

> **May your hearts be fully committed to the LORD our God, to live by his decrees and obey his commands.**
>
> 1 Kings 8:61

Introduction
God wants us to keep showing our love of and obedience to Him. Let's find out about one man who had to patiently keep doing what God wanted him to do.

Presentation

1. Invite volunteers to examine the Bibles you collected. **In what ways are these books alike? How are they different?** Accept responses. **Today the Bible has been written in many different languages so people all over the world can read God's Word. But back in the 1500s, the Bible English-speaking people had was written in Latin. Because only a few people could understand Latin, most people couldn't read God's Word for themselves.**

2. One man named William Tyndale, however, wanted people to have Bibles they could read. William was a teacher who lived in England. But the leaders in England didn't want people to be able to read the Bible for themselves! William didn't let that stop him. He understood Latin, so he carefully translated the New Testament into English. Soon people all over England were buying and reading this English New Testament. The leaders, however, were so angry they bought all the English New Testaments they could find and burned them! William was very discouraged. But then he heard some good news. The money William had earned from selling the English New Testaments to the angry leaders was enough to print even more New Testaments than before! William Tyndale patiently worked to print the English New Testaments over again so that people once again could read God's Word.

Conclusion
Read 1 Kings 8:61 aloud. **When we are "committed to the Lord," it means we patiently keep doing what's right, even when it's hard. What did William Tyndale do, even though it was hard?** (He translated the New Testament into English. He sold copies of the New Testament so he could print more.) **God promises to help us.** Lead children in prayer, asking God for helpt to patiently continue to obey Him.

Discussion Questions

1. **What do you think it means to commit our hearts to God?** (to love God more than anyone or anything) **How will this help us to do the right thing?** (When we are committed to God, we want to please Him in everything we do.)

2. **What are some of the things we know God wants us to do?** (show love to others, speak kind words to others, tell the truth, pray to Him) **When would kids your age need patience to keep doing those good things?** (when they don't feel like being kind, when people aren't being kind to them, when people make fun of them)

3. **What is another word for doing what God wants you to do?** (obeying) **When is a time it might be hard to patiently keep obeying God?** (when friends ask you to do something you know is wrong, or they don't care if you do the right thing or not)

4. **What are some things you can do to keep doing what God wants you to do?** (pray to God for His help, talk with others who love God)

Discussion Questions

William Tyndale's first New Testament was printed in 1526. About ten years later, William was killed because he had translated the Bible. Then within five years of his death, the king of England approved another English Bible (based on William's translation) and required every church to make copies available to the people!

The Shelter

God's Word helps us learn how to have self-control and live wisely.

Materials
- Bible with a bookmark at Psalm 119:133
- umbrella

> **Direct my footsteps according to your word; let no sin rule over me.**
> Psalm 119:133

Introduction
God's Word helps us learn how to have self-control and live wisely. Listen to find out about one man and his family who helped others learn about God's Word too!

Presentation
1. Show the umbrella. **When do people use this? Why?** Accept responses. **People use an umbrella for shelter from rain and snow. A man named Francis Schaeffer and his family named their home in Switzerland L'Abri** (lah-BREE), **the French word for "the shelter." Why might you call a home a shelter?** (keeps you safe)

2. **Francis Schaeffer and his family moved from America to Switzerland because they wanted to help people in Europe learn about God. They knew that many Europeans had questions about God and the Bible. Francis and his family wanted to help people discover the answers to their questions by teaching them about God's Word. The Schaeffer family made their house, L'Abri, a place where people from around the world could come and study God's Word. They prayed God would send to L'Abri people who had questions about God. While the Schaeffers' guests lived at L'Abri, they saw how people who loved God lived each day. The Schaeffers helped their guests learn wisdom from the Bible. Many of these guests became convinced God is real and that His Word tells the best way to live.**

Conclusion
Read Psalm 119:133 aloud. **What does it mean for God to direct your footsteps according to God's Word?** (He will help you obey the Bible.) **What did the Schaeffer family do that showed they obeyed God's Word?** (They opened their home to teach others about God.) **God's Word teaches us wise ways to live, and as we follow these wise ways, we learn to have self-control.** Lead children in prayer, thanking God for His Word that tells us wise ways to live.

Discussion Questions

1. **What are some of the ways God's Word tells us to live?** (love and forgive others, ask Jesus to forgive our sins, pray to God and ask for help with our problems, tell the good news about Jesus to other people)

2. **What is one way you can obey God's Word this week?** Share your own answer with your children before asking them to respond.

Additional Information for Older Children

When Francis Schaeffer was a teenager, he decided he didn't know whether God really existed or not. Francis began to read the Bible to find out. Francis started reading in the book of Genesis. After reading the Bible, Francis became convinced that God is real. Francis also believed that the Bible is God's Word. Francis became a Christian when he was 18 years old, and for the rest of his life he helped others learn to believe in God.

Weeks of Celebration
God's Word tells us the best way to live.

Materials
- Bible with bookmarks at Leviticus 23:17 and Psalm 119:66
- 2 loaves of bread
- honey
- softened cream cheese (8 oz.)
- small bowl
- plastic knives
- napkins

Introduction

We can learn the best way to live by studying God's Word. People in the Old Testament celebrated a holiday that reminded them of the time when God gave His law to Moses. They called this holiday the Feast of Weeks. Let's find out how the holiday was named and what the people did to celebrate it.

Presentation

1. **The Feast (or Festival) of Weeks is celebrated seven weeks plus one day after the Passover celebration. Another name for this holiday is Shavuot** (shah-voo-OHT), **which is the Hebrew word for "weeks."**

2. **At this celebration, God told His people that two loaves of bread were to be waved as an offering, or gift, to God.** Wave the loaves of bread in the air as a demonstration. Read or ask an older child to read Leviticus 23:17. **At this time of the year, the harvest of grains used to make bread had just been completed, and the people were glad to thank God for the food they would make from the grains.**

3. **Today the two loaves of bread remind us of the two tablets on which God wrote the Ten Commandments He gave to Moses. God gave the Ten Commandments so His people would have His Word to help them. During the Feast of Weeks today, Jewish people read the Ten Commandments aloud.**

4. **During the Feast of Weeks, it is also traditional to eat dairy products as reminders of God's Word, which is "sweet" because it gives us what we need to grow in our knowledge of God.** Mix small amounts of honey with cream cheese to form a spread. Spread the mixture on bread. Cut the bread into quarters and serve.

Conclusion

Now we have more than the Ten Commandments to help us learn the best way to live. We have the whole Bible to help us! Read Psalm 119:66 aloud. **To have good judgment means to be wise and know the right things to do and say. We know we can depend on God to help us be wise and make good choices.** Pray, asking God's help in doing what's right.

Discussion Questions

1. **What are some of the commands God gives us in the Bible?** (love God more than anything, love your neighbor, forgive each other, do not lie, do not steal, honor your parents, treat others fairly, say kind words)

2. **What is one way you can follow these commands this week?** Volunteers can respond.

3. **When you need help following God's commands, what can you do?** (ask God for help to obey, talk to your mom or dad about what to do)

Additional Information for Older Children

The Bible uses word pictures to describe God's Word and the ways in which it helps us. Children can find and read these verses in their Bibles: Psalm 12:6; 19:9–10; 119:103, 105.

You've Got Mail!

The Bible is God's true story, and reading it helps us know and love Him.

Materials

- Bag into which you have placed a Bible with a bookmark at John 20:31
- variety of mail (bill, letter, greeting card, advertisement, catalog, email, magazine, etc.)

> **These are written that you may believe that Jesus is the Messiah, the Son of God, and that by believing you may have life in his name.**
>
> John 20:31

Introduction

The Bible is like a letter from God—written just to me and you. In this bag I have a sample of some of the mail I received this week. As I take the mail out of the bag, let's talk about how God's letter is different from the rest of the mail.

Presentation

1. One at a time, hold up each piece of mail (keeping the Bible until the last) and ask volunteers to describe each. Discuss by asking questions such as, **Who is this mail from? What is this mail trying to get me to do? What message does this mail tell me? Why might I be excited to get this mail?**

2. Hold up the Bible. **How would you describe this letter? How is God's letter to us different from the rest of the mail I've received?** (It was written long ago. Its message is for everyone.) **What makes God's Word better than any other message to us?** (It's true. It tells the good news about Jesus.)

Conclusion

Read John 20:31 aloud. **The words in the Bible help each person learn that when we believe Jesus is God's Son, we can be part of God's family.** Talk with interested children about becoming Christians (see "Leading a Child to Christ," p. 8). Thank God for sending His letter to each of us, and ask His help in getting to know more about Him as we read the Bible.

Discussion Questions

1. What's your favorite kind of mail?

2. What's the best thing you've ever received in the mail?

3. When are some times you read God's letter—the Bible?

Guidance from God

Bible Translators

Have a gentle attitude so you can learn wisdom from God and others who love Him.

Listen to advice and accept discipline, and at the end you will be counted among the wise.

Proverbs 19:20

Materials
- Bible with a bookmark at Proverbs 19:20
- object representing something a friend has taught you or helped you with (golf club, crocheted blanket, paintbrush, pie tin, etc.)
- Wycliffe guest or information *(optional)*

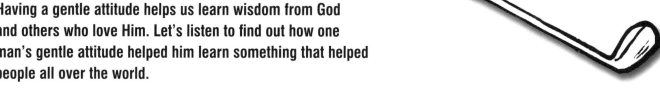

Introduction
Having a gentle attitude helps us learn wisdom from God and others who love Him. Let's listen to find out how one man's gentle attitude helped him learn something that helped people all over the world.

Presentation
1. Show and describe the object. **I brought this (golf club) because my friend _____ (friend's name) helped me learn how to (play golf). What is something a friend has helped you learn?** Let children respond. **A man named Cameron Townsend went to Guatemala as a missionary. He was very glad to find a friend there to help him.**

2. **When Cameron first went to Guatemala, whenever he met people with whom he wanted to talk about God, he'd ask, "Do you know the Lord Jesus?" But when he asked this question in Spanish, it translated as, "Do you know Mr. Jesus (hay-SOOS)?" Because Jesus is a common Hispanic name, the people he was talking to did not know Cameron was talking about Jesus the Son of God. He also discovered that many of the people he talked to did not even know Spanish but spoke other languages. There were hundreds of different languages in that area! Cameron wondered how he would be able to talk to these people about Jesus, so he prayed for God's help. Soon Cameron met an Indian named Francisco Diaz who loved God too. Francisco taught Cameron his language and helped him translate the New Testament into that language. Cameron was so excited about this idea of translating the Scriptures into everyone's own language that he began an organization called Wycliffe Bible Translators. Today, Wycliffe missionaries help people all over the world learn about God in their own language, all because of God's help and Cameron Townsend's willingness to learn from Francisco.**

Conclusion

Read Proverbs 19:20 aloud. **This verse describes what someone who has a gentle attitude is like. The word** *discipline* **here has the meaning of "instruction." What did Cameron Townsend learn because he had a gentle attitude and accepted instruction?** (He learned to speak the language of the people he wanted to help.) Lead children in prayer, asking God's help in learning from others.

Discussion Questions

1. **What other words can you use to describe someone who has a gentle attitude?** (listens, humble, peaceful, respectful, unselfish)

2. **Why does having a gentle attitude lead to wisdom?** (Listening to others is a way to learn from them.) Ask a volunteer to read Proverbs 19:20 aloud.

3. **Who are some good people to learn from?** (parents, people who love God, teachers, pastors) **What can you learn from (teachers) when you have a gentle attitude?** (how to love God and others, right choices, and ways to obey God)

4. **What are some ways you can get instructions from God?** (read God's Word, pray to Him, talk to other people who love God)

Additional Information for Older Children

Wycliffe Bible missionaries have translated the New Testament into more than 500 languages, and they work in more than 70 countries. The average translation job takes 10 to 20 years! *(Optional: Invite someone who has served with Wycliffe to talk to your children, or find additional information online.)*

Birthday Candles

God gives us the Holy Spirit to guide us and to help us tell others about Jesus.

> He proclaimed the kingdom of God and taught about the Lord Jesus Christ—with all boldness and without hindrance!
>
> Acts 28:31

Materials

- Bible with a bookmark at Acts 28:31
- birthday candles
- small cake or cupcake, matches *(optional)*

Introduction

The Holy Spirit was given to us by God in order to guide us and help us tell others about Jesus. Let's look at a way to remember the special day the Holy Spirit came to the disciples.

Presentation

1. Display the candles you brought. **How are candles used on birthdays? What do the number of candles on a birthday cake often show?** Accept responses. *(Optional: Place candles one a small cake or cupcake. Light the candles and allow children to blow them out.)*

2. **On one day every year, the birthday of God's church is celebrated. This day is called Pentecost. The word** *pentecost* **means "50." Pentecost takes place 50 days after the Passover celebration. In Bible times, Jesus' disciples had come to Jerusalem after Jesus had gone to heaven. While they were there, God sent His Holy Spirit to the disciples. This day is celebrated as the beginning of God's church.**

Conclusion

The Holy Spirit is still with us, helping us to love and obey God. Read Acts 28:31 aloud. **What does it mean to do something "with all boldness and without hindrance"?** (to not be afraid, to be brave and confident) *T*his verse is talking about Paul. **The Holy Spirit helped Paul tell others about Jesus. The Holy Spirit will help us too! All we have to do is ask.** Pray, thanking God for His gift of the Holy Spirit and asking for His guidance and help as we tell others about Jesus.

Discussion Questions

1. **What happened when God first sent the Holy Spirit?** (The disciples spoke in different languages. Jesus' followers became the first church.)

2. **Why did God send the Holy Spirit?** (to help members of His family love and obey Him)

3. **What are some ways the Holy Spirit can help us?** (The Holy Spirit guides us in knowing the right things to do, reminds us of and helps us follow God's commands in the Bible, and helps us know the words to say when we tell others about Jesus.)

Additional Information for Older Children

The first Sunday after Pentecost is called Trinity Sunday. On this day, some churches celebrate the holy Trinity, the fact that God is made up of three persons: God the Father, God the Son, and God the Holy Spirit. One of the objects used to represent the holy Trinity is the candle, because a candle is made up of three parts: the wax, the wick, and the flame. Have the children read Jesus' words about the Holy Spirit in John 15:26.

Gifts to Honor
God gives us people to guide and care for us.

Materials
- Bible with bookmarks at Exodus 20:12 and Proverbs 3:5–6
- several gifts traditionally given on Mother's Day (candy, flowers, cards, etc.)

> **Trust in the LORD with all your heart and lean not on your own understanding; in all your ways submit to him, and he will make your paths straight.**
>
> Proverbs 3:5–6

Introduction
One of the ways God cares for us is by giving us people to guide and care for us. Let's look at ways we can honor these people who are gifts from God.

Presentation
1. One at a time, display the gifts you brought. **Who might you give this gift to? Why would you give this gift?** Repeat for each of the gifts you brought.

2. **On Mother's Day, we give gifts like these to mothers and other people who care for us.** Read Exodus 20:12 aloud. **Giving gifts is one way to honor people who care for us and let them know we appreciate all that they do for us. There are lots of types of mothers—grandmothers, stepmothers, foster mothers, and people who act like mothers! They are all given to us by God to guide and care for us. Who are some other people God has given to care for you?** (fathers, aunts, older brothers or sisters, teachers) Invite volunteers to tell ways people care for them.

3. **This year on Mother's Day, you can honor your mother or anyone else who guides you and cares for you. What are some special or unusual ways to honor this person?** (say "I love you," give a back massage, water flowers, clean your room and bathroom, cook dinner)

Conclusion
Read Proverbs 3:5–6 aloud. According to these verses, whose directions should we follow? (God's directions) **How can we know what God wants us to do?** (by reading God's Word and listening to parents and other people who guide and care for us) Pray, thanking God that He gives us people to guide and care for us.

Discussion Questions

1. Who are the people you want to honor today? How do they guide and care for you?

2. What are some ways we need to be cared for? What are some good reasons to have people to guide us?
   (to help us know what to do in our lives, to teach us good ways to live)

3. Who are some people who teach you about God? What can you do to thank God for giving you people to guide you in knowing Him?

Additional Information for Older Children

Mother's Day in the United States was first suggested by Julia Ward Howe (who wrote the words to the "Battle Hymn of the Republic") in 1872; the holiday was first celebrated nationally in 1914. Other countries around the world (such as France) have also established spring days to honor mothers. England observes Mothering Sunday, a custom dating back to the Middle Ages when worshippers returned to their "mother" churches for special services.

It Is Well

Rely on God's wisdom and show patience, even when bad things we don't understand happen.

> **Trust in the LORD with all your heart and lean not on your own understanding.**
>
> Proverbs 3:5

Materials

- Bible with abookmark at Proverbs 3:5
- sheet of paper
- pencil
- hymnbook with "It Is Well with My Soul," a musician to lead children in singing the hymn *(optional)*

Introduction

When bad things happen we don't understand, sometimes the hardest thing to do is trust God's wisdom and show patience. But that is actually the best thing to do! Let's find out how one man trusted God's wisdom when something terrible happened to his family.

Presentation

1. Hold up the paper and pencil. **What do you usually do with these two objects?** Children can respond. **A man named Horatio Spafford used a pencil and paper to write a poem to express how he was feeling.**

2. **In 1873 Horatio Spafford sent his wife and four daughters ahead of him on a ship to Europe while he completed some unexpected business. Soon he received a message from his wife that the ship had sunk and all their daughters died. Only his wife survived. Horatio quickly got on a ship and sailed to meet his wife. As his ship was passing the spot where his daughters had drowned, Horatio went out on the deck and wrote these words: "When sorrows like sea billows roll—whatever my lot, Thou hast taught me to say, it is well, it is well with my soul."** *(Optional: Read the entire first verse of the hymn aloud.)*

3. **What do you think he meant by writing "it is well with my soul"?** Accept responses. **Horatio wrote that whether he felt peace or sorrow, he trusted God. People were so impressed with the words of Horatio's poem they put the poem to music, and it became a popular hymn people still sing today.** *(Optional: Have a musician lead the children in singing the hymn.)* Lead children in prayer, thanking God that we can trust Him with our problems, no matter how bad the problems are.

Conclusion

Read Proverbs 3:5 aloud. **How did Horatio Spafford show he trusted in God, even when bad things happened to him?** (He wrote a song about loving and trusting God.)

Discussion Questions

1. **What might help you show patience during hard times?** (talking to God about the situation, praying and asking God for patience, reading the Bible to find out how God helped people in all kinds of hard situations)

2. **How does knowing that God is wise make it easier to be patient in hard times?** (God knows what we need and will give it to us at just the right time. He plans everything for our good. He has a reason for everything.)

3. **What are some things you can do to remember God's wisdom in order to help you show patience?** (talk to God, read about how God helped people in the Bible, talk to others about times they relied on God's wisdom)

Additional Information for Older Children

After the accident, the Spaffords had more children. They also moved to Israel. Years passed, and their daughter, Bertha, grew up. One day a Muslim man whose wife had died asked Bertha to raise his newborn baby. Soon many people were bringing children whose parents had left them, and so began what is now called the Spafford Children's Center. God helped the Spafford family and their staff raise as many as 60 children at a time!

Quick Change
Listen to God your whole life.

Materials
Bible with a bookmark at Exodus 15:26

Introduction
Sometimes you might think that only grown-ups need to listen to God. But God wants everyone—for their whole lives—to listen to Him. When you listen to someone, it's important to pay careful attention to what the person says and does. Let's find out how good we are at paying attention.

Presentation
1. Ask children to look at you for 10 seconds, paying attention to the details of how you are dressed.

2. Ask children to close their eyes (or you may briefly step out of the room). Quickly change one detail about how you are dressed (remove glasses, take off a sweater, roll up sleeves, etc.).

3. Ask the children to carefully look at you again, trying to identify the change you made. After change is identified or after 30 seconds, repeat the activity, letting volunteers make changes to their appearance. Vary the difficulty of changes made according to the age of your children. As children are guessing changes, comment occasionally about the way in which they are paying careful attention.

Conclusion
Read Exodus 15:26 aloud. **What does this verse say about litening and paying careful attention? Listening to God's voice helps us know how to love and obey Him. We can listen to God's voice as we read and hear Bible stories and as we pray to Him.** Lead children in prayer, asking God's help in listening to Him and doing what's right in His eyes.

Discussion Questions

1. **Who are some people you listen to?**

2. **When might it be hard to remember to listen to God?** (when someone wants you to do wrong)

3. **Who are some people who help you listen to God?**

4. **How can you help others listen to God?** (pray for them, talk with them about what you read in God's Word)

What's Dependable?

No matter how bad things look, depend on God because He is in control.

Materials

- Bible with a bookmark at Jeremiah 17:7
- a variety of familiar objects (alarm clock, ruler, pen, flashlight, dictionary, measuring cup, TV remote, etc.)

Introduction

We all need help when we have problems, feel worried, or don't know what to do. God's Word tells us that in any situation we can be confident that God will help us. Let's find out why we can depend on God more than any object or person.

Presentation

Show each object one at a time. Invite volunteers to answer these questions about each object: **What is this object used for? When have you used this object? How did this object help you? Why can you depend on this item to help you? When can't you depend on this item to help you?**

Conclusion

Even though these items can help us and give us true information in many situations, sometimes they can't help us. Listen to this Bible verse to find out whom we can depend on in *any* situation, no matter how bad things look. Read Jeremiah 17:7 aloud. **Why can we be confident in God's help?** (He is more powerful than anything in the world. He loves us and promises to be with us.) Lead children in prayer, thanking God for His help and that He is always with us.

Discussion Questions

1. **What are some other objects you depend on?** (car, bike, computer) **Why might these items not always be dependable?** (cars break down, bikes get flat tires, computers crash)

2. **What are some times when kids your age need to depend on God's help? How about people older than you? Younger than you?**

3. **What can you do when you need to remember God's help?** (pray to Him, remember a Bible verse about His power and help)

Wise Ways

God's gift of wisdom helps us know the best way to live.

Materials
- Bible with a bookmark at Proverbs 2:6
- variety of lists (grocery list, phone book, chore list, encyclopedia, dictionary, etc.)
- large sheet of paper or whiteboard, marker *(optional)*

> **The LORD gives wisdom; from his mouth come knowledge and understanding.**
> Proverbs 2:6

Introduction
If we ask God, He will give us wisdom to know the best way to live. When people celebrate the coming of a new year, they often think about better ways to live. Let's talk about how some people remind themselves of wise ways to live.

Presentation

1. Give each list you brought to a volunteer to describe. **What kind of list is this? How does this list help the person who wrote it or who is reading it? What kinds of lists do you or the people in your family make?** Accept responses.

2. **As part of their New Year's Day celebrations, some people make lists called New Year's resolutions. A resolution is something you plan or promise to do. When people write New Year's resolutions, they usually list wise ways of living.** (*Optional: Ask children to tell items often listed as New Year's resolutions.*)

3. **We can always think of good ways to live, such as eating healthy food or getting enough sleep. But because God loves us so much, He gives us the help we need to live the very best way. What are some ways we can find out the very best ways to live?** (ask God for wisdom, read God's Word, listen to advice from people who love and obey God) Volunteers can read Proverbs 10:8; 10:12; 12:18; 15:1; and 17:17 for additional ideas. (*Optional: On a large sheet of paper or whiteboard, have children list wise ways to live that each begin with one of the letters in the words* Happy New Year.)

Conclusion
Read Proverbs 2:6 aloud. **What are some wise actions God will help us learn?** (how to show His love to others, how to be a good friend) Pray, praising God for His gift of wisdom and asking for His help to live in wise ways.

Discussion Questions

1. **What are some times when kids your age need to be wise?** (when tempted to do something wrong, when making a choice about how to treat others)

2. **The Bible tells us that God gives us wisdom. How can we get wisdom from God?** (ask God to help us make wise decisions and then trust Him to answer our prayers, think about what God's Word says to do and how to obey it)

3. **What does the Bible say are some wise ways to live?** (love others, be kind, tell the truth, be generous to others) **Why is it wise to live those ways?**

Additional Information for Older Children

King Solomon was known throughout the world for his wisdom. He wrote several books in the Bible, including Ecclesiastes. Ecclesiastes 3:1–13 is a list of different things that may happen to people. These verses are sometimes read at New Year's services. Let volunteers read Ecclesiastes 3:1–13 aloud.

Help from God

Anger Control

God can help us control angry feelings so we can treat others in ways that please Him.

> **Fools give full vent to their rage, but the wise bring calm in the end.**
>
> Proverbs 29:11

Materials
- Bible with a bookmark at Proverbs 29:11
- month-by-month calendar
- copy of "I Have a Dream" speech by Dr. Martin Luther King Jr. *(optional)*

Introduction
With God's help, we can treat others in ways that pleases Him, even when we're angry. Let's find out what one man did to control angry feelings.

Presentation

1. Invite several volunteers to find favorite holidays listed on the calendar. **What or who do these holidays help us to remember?** Invite responses. **Martin Luther King Jr. is a man whose actions are remembered each year by many people.**

2. **Martin Luther King Jr. Day is celebrated each year on the third Monday of January. What do you know about Dr. King?** Supplement the children's information as needed with the following: **In 1954 Dr. King became the pastor of a church in Alabama. At this time many African American people felt very angry because they weren't being treated fairly. Dr. King was angry too. Dr. King believed that because God loves everyone the same, all people should be treated fairly. Even though he was angry, Martin Luther King Jr. didn't let his angry feelings cause him to treat others in unkind ways. Instead, he led marches to call attention to unfairness. He gave speeches and preached sermons, telling people to treat each other fairly. Dr. King asked government leaders to pass laws so African Americans would be treated fairly. He also warned people to do what was right at all times and to treat others in ways that pleased God.** *(Optional: Read aloud part of Dr. King's "I Have a Dream" speech.)*

Conclusion

Read Proverbs 29:11 aloud. **What does Proverbs 29:11 say a wise person does?** Accept answers. **When we keep our words and actions under control, it means we think about and plan our words and actions so that they show love and obedience to God. What is a way Martin Luther King Jr. showed he had self-control?** (He didn't treat others in unkind ways, even when he was angry. He taught others to do right and please God.) Lead children in prayer, asking God to help them show self-control.

Discussion Questions

1. **When are some times it is hard for kids your age to control their anger?**

2. **What are some things people do to help control their anger?** (count to ten, take a deep breath, walk away, tell God about their anger, ask God's help in being kind)

3. **Why do you think it is wise to control your anger?**

Additional Information for Older Children

In 1964 Martin Luther King Jr. won the Nobel Peace Prize. Every year, beginning in 1901, money set aside by a Swedish inventor, Alfred Nobel, is divided; and five prizes are given to people who have worked hard to help others. There are awards for the most important discovery or invention in physics, chemistry, and medicine—as well as awards for literature and working for international peace. Martin Luther King Jr. won the prize for peace because he taught people to live peacefully with each other.

Choosing Self-Control
Depending on God for self-control helps us make good choices.

Materials
- Bible with a bookmark at 1 Corinthians 16:13
- 1 or more ears of corn (if possible, bring corn still in the husk)

> **Be on your guard; stand firm in the faith; be courageous; be strong.**
>
> 1 Corinthians 16:13

Introduction
Asking God for help with self-control can help us make good choices.
Let's find out about someone who depended on God's help and made good choices.

Presentation
1. Show the ear(s) of corn. **We usually eat the corn and throw the husk and the cob away. One man, Peter Cartwright, used an entire cornstalk to show self-control and to help another person do the same thing.**

2. In the early part of the 1800s, many families in America lived far from each other. One of the few times these families would get together was when a traveling preacher, like Peter Cartwright, came to visit. Each time Peter came to an area where several families lived, he led church meetings and talked with the families about God. After one of these church meetings, Peter was invited to dinner at a nearby home. One of the men at the dinner was angry with Peter, because he thought Peter had treated the man's son unfairly. The man challenged Peter to a duel to the death! Peter could have became angry with the man. Instead he said, "According to the rules of honor, I have the right to choose the weapon. Isn't that right?" The man nodded. Peter smiled and said, "Let's go outside and grab a couple of cornstalks to fight with. I think that ought to settle things. Don't you?" The other man started to laugh and realized he didn't need to be so angry. Soon the argument ended. At the next church meeting, the man became a member of God's family.

Conclusion
Read 1 Corinthians 16:13 aloud. **How did Peter Cartwright obey this verse?** (Peter didn't get angry. He helped the other man do what was right.) **How did his self-control help to avoid trouble?** Let the children respond. Lead children in prayer, asking for God's help to have self-control and make good choices. **One good choice we all can make is to become members of God's family.** Talk with interested children about becoming members of God's family (see "Leading a Child to Christ" on p. 8).

Discussion Questions

1. When do you think a kid your age needs self-control?

2. When were some specific times you needed to have self-control? How did your self-control help the situation? What might have happened if you didn't have self-control?

3. What can you do when you need self-control and the ability to make good choices? (pray to God and ask for His help, remember Bible verses that tell about God's help)

Additional Information for Older Children

Peter Cartwright hated slavery. In 1824 he moved his family to the state of Illinois. In Illinois it was against the law to own slaves. Peter Cartwright decided to become a government leader and won many elections. His only defeat was in 1846 when he lost an election for the Unites States Congress to Abraham Lincoln! Peter Cartwright wrote the story of his life in the book *Autobiography of Peter Cartwright, the Backwoods Preacher*.

Delicious Decorations

Remembering God's goodness throughout our lives makes us want to celebrate the ways He cares for us.

Materials

- Bible with a bookmark at Romans 8:28
- several types of fruits and vegetables
- large bag
- 1 or more blindfolds
- knife

> **We know that in all things God works for the good of those who love him.**
>
> Romans 8:28

Preparation

Place the fruits and vegetables in a large bag.

Introduction

When we remember God's goodness throughout our lives, we want to celebrate His care. During Old Testament times God's people celebrated the Feast (or Festival) of Tabernacles (or Booths), called Sukkot (suh-KOHT) in Hebrew, as a reminder of the good things God provides for His people. Let's discover some of the things they used in their celebration.

Presentation

1. Read Deuteronomy 16:13–15 aloud. **What did the people build during the Feast of Tabernacles? Why?** (God's people built booths to remind them of God's care for their ancestors while they traveled in the desert on their way to the Promised Land.) **Try to discover what items people in our city might use to decorate a booth during the Feast of Tabernacles—which Jewish people still celebrate.**

2. Blindfold a volunteer. Take out one fruit or vegetable from bag. The volunteer tries to identify the food only by touching it. If the volunteer cannot identify food by touching it, suggest he or she smell and then taste bite-size pieces of the food. As time allows, repeat with new volunteers for each fruit and vegetable. **During Sukkot, the booths are decorated with fruits and vegetables as a reminder of the good things God provides for His people.**

Conclusion

Fruits and vegetables are only a few of the good things God has given to His people. Read Romans 8:28 aloud. **This verse tells us God always cares for us no matter what happens. What are some of the ways God has cared for you?** Pray, thanking God for the things mentioned in any responses. Close the prayer by praising God for His goodness to us.

Discussion Questions

1. **What are some ways to celebrate God's goodness?** (thank Him when you pray, treat others with the same goodness God shows to you, tell people about God's goodness, sing songs of praise to Him)

2. **What does God show us about himself by caring for us?** (He loves us. He is good.)

3. **How does God show His goodness to us in hard times?** (He keeps His promises to us.)

4. **What are some of the ways people today celebrate God's care?** (thank Him in prayer, make banners or write prayers about God's care)

Additional Information for Older Children

The Feast of Tabernacles was one of three important holidays God instructed His people to celebrate. In Bible times, God's people (called Hebrews or Israelites) traveled to Jerusalem for these three celebrations. As they traveled, they sang songs from the book of Psalms. Psalm 120–134 are called the Psalms of Ascent. The word *ascent* means to be rising or climbing up toward something. Invite volunteers to read aloud the first verse of each psalm in Psalm 120–123.

Games to Go
We can trust in God's promises to guide and protect us.

Materials
- Bible with bookmarks at Psalm 121 and Jeremiah 17:7
- travel games (travel-size board games, magnetic checker and chess sets, etc.)

> **Blessed is the one who trusts in the Lord, whose confidence is in him.**
> Jeremiah 17:7

Introduction
With God's help, we can treat others in ways that please Him, even when we're angry. Let's find out what one man did to control angry feelings.

Presentation
1. **Show the travel games. When might you play a game like this?** Accept responses. **What games do you play on trips with your family?** (Twenty Questions, the Alphabet Game, etc.) **What songs might you sing when you travel?** ("Bingo," "Old MacDonald," etc.) *(Optional: Sing the songs or play the games children suggest.)*

2. **In Old Testament times, the people sang songs when they traveled, just like we do. Many of these songs are written for us in the book of Psalms.** Ask a volunteer to read the phrase written under the Psalm 121 heading in the Bible: "A song of ascents." **The word *ascent* means to go or move upwards. This phrase means the psalm was sung during a yearly trip called a pilgrimage to Jerusalem. Jerusalem and the temple were located higher up on a mountain than most of the other towns in Israel, so the people would travel up to Jerusalem in order to worship God in the temple. As they traveled, there must have been times when God's people were scared or worried. Singing this song reminded them of God's promises to love, guide, and protect them.** Read or ask an older child to read Psalm 121.

Conclusion
Wherever we go, we can remember God's promises to guide and protect us too. Read Jeremiah 17:7 aloud. **Who does this verse tell us is blessed?** (anyone who trusts God) **Who can give us confidence?** (the Lord) Pray, praising God for His guidance and protection and thanking Him we can trust in Him to keep us safe wherever we go.

Discussion Questions

1. **How do your parents or teachers give you guidance or instruction?** (tell what to do, write lists, show how to do things)

2. **When are some times kids your age need to pray and trust God for His guidance and protection?** (when there are hard jobs to do at home or at school, when others do mean things)

3. **In what ways does God guide us?** (by His instructions in the Bible, by giving us people who tell us the right ways to love God and others, by answering our prayers)

4. **What are some ways to show we trust God to be our guide?** (ask His help when making choices, read God's Word to discover His commands)

Additional Information for Older Children

Just as we have different songs for different holidays and other occasions, people in Old Testament times had many different kinds of songs. The word *psalms* means "praises." The book of Psalms is actually 150 songs. Many of them are songs of praise to God. Psalms 120–134 are called Psalms of Ascent and are also known as the pilgrimage psalms because people sang them while going from one place to another.

House Afire
Wait patiently and depend on God to keep His promises.

Materials

- Bible with a bookmark at Psalm 33:20
- an item from your home you would want to save in the event of a fire
- copy of the poem "Upon the Burning of Our House" by Anne Bradstreet *(optional)*

> **We wait in hope for the LORD; he is our help and our shield.**
>
> Psalm 33:20

Introduction

Because we know God will always keep His promises, we can be patient and depend on Him. Let's find out how one person showed hope and trust in God's promises

Presentation

1. **What would you try to save if your house caught on fire?** Accept responses. **Then show the item that you brought. This is something I would not want to lose in a fire.** Explain why the item is important to you. **A woman named Anne Bradstreet realized that something else was important when her house burned down.**

2. **Anne Bradstreet, her husband, and her parents sailed on a boat from England to America in 1630. They began living in the Massachusetts Bay Colony. One night, Anne woke up to the sounds of a fire. Anne and her family escaped the blaze, but they couldn't save anything in their house. The entire house and everything in it were destroyed! Anne wrote a poem about her feelings when her home burned. In the poem, Anne said she would miss the many things that were destroyed, but the things most important to her—God's promises—could not be burned. Anne believed God's promises were her most important treasures. Through her poem, Anne showed that she trusted God to care for her family and that she chose to hope and trust in God's promises.** *(Optional: Read "Upon the Burning of Our House" aloud.)*

Conclusion

Read Psalm 33:20 aloud. **How did Anne Bradstreet show hope in God? Why do you think Anne chose to respond the way she did?** Let children respond. **Let's ask God to help us remember to depend on His promises and be patient.** Lead children in prayer.

Discussion Questions

1. **What are some promises you know God has made? What do you know about God that would make you trust Him to keep His promises?**

2. **What might help us wait patiently for God to keep His promises?** (remembering the times He has helped us in the past, thanking Him for His love for us, praying and asking Him for patience)

3. **What are some of God's promises for which we never have to wait?** (God's promise to always be with us, God's promise to give us courage)

Additional Information for Older Children

During the time when Anne Bradstreet lived, few women could read or write, let alone write poems! But when Anne was growing up, her father had worked for an important man in England. Because her father had such an important job, he was able to pay people to teach Anne how to play music and how to speak and write several languages. Later on, after she had moved to America, Anne used her talent for writing to describe her love for her husband, her children, and most of all, her love for God.

Joy in the Pit
Joyfully celebrate God's help and protection.

Materials
- Bible with a bookmark at Psalm 92:4
- shovel

Introduction
We can joyfully celebrate God's help and protection! Let's find out about a man who celebrated God at every opportunity he had!

Presentation

1. Ask a volunteer to demonstrate how to use a shovel. **What are some hard jobs people have to do with shovels?** (dig ditches, dig in fields, dig big holes) **A man named George Chen had to dig with a shovel every day for more than five years doing a job no one else wanted!**

2. **George Chen lived in China and was sent to prison because he was a Christian and came from a wealthy family. In that prison, no one was allowed to talk about God, read a Bible, or pray. Each person in the prison had a job to do. George's job was to shovel out the huge hole in the ground where all the waste from the prison was put. Each day the guards lowered George and his shovel into the pit. All day long George worked hard. Most people would have hated such a smelly, dirty job! But George soon discovered that because the pit was so dirty and smelly, no guards came to check on him while he worked. Every day George was free to sing songs of praise to God, to pray out loud, and to recite Bible verses he had memorized. If he had worked inside the prison in a cleaner place, he would not have been able to sing and pray aloud! George joyfully thanked God—even when it was hard!**

Conclusion
Read Psalm 92:4 aloud. **When was George Chen able to sing to God and praise Him? We don't have to wait to be alone or in a smelly pit to sing and praise God! We can praise Him anytime!** Lead children in prayer, praising God for specific actions He has done (creating the world, forgiving our sins, answering our prayers).

Discussion Questions

1. **When has God helped or protected you or someone you know?** Share an age-appropriate example of your own before asking children to answer.

2. **When are some times a kid your age might need God's help and protection?** (during a thunderstorm, when going to a new school, when standing up for what's right)

3. **What are some ways to show your joy and celebrate God's help and protection?** (sing songs of praise to God, pray to thank God for all He has done, tell others about how God helps and protects His people)

4. **Why do you think praising God brings us joy?** (We are happy He has cared for us and promises always to care for us. It pleases God when we praise Him. It reminds us of His love and faithfulness. It makes us love Him more.)

Additional Information for Older Children

George Chen spent 18 years in the prison. When he was set free, he helped Chinese Christians start new churches and tell other people about Jesus. During the years George was in prison, the government killed many Chinese Christians who were not in prison. George thanked God that because he was in prison for so long, he was kept alive, and he could continue to obey God after he was set free.

Passover Power

Whenever we need help, we can depend on God's power.

Materials
- Bible with bookmarks at Exodus 12:24–27 and Psalm 46:1
- bite-size pieces of unleavened bread (or matzo crackers)
- bread prepared with yeast
- 2 paper plates

> **If any of you lacks wisdom, you should ask God, who gives generously to all without finding fault, and it will be given to you.**
>
> James 1:5

Preparation
Put each type of bread on a different plate.

Introduction
We can depend on God's power whenever we need help. Long ago in Old Testament times, God helped the Israelites escape from slavery in Egypt. Let's find out how God told His people to remember and celebrate His great power and help.

Presentation
1. **As part of this celebration God told His people to eat a special kind of bread.** Let children eat samples of each type of bread. **What are the differences you can find by touching and tasting the two different kinds of bread?** Volunteers can respond. Identify which is unleavened bread. **Because unleavened bread does not have yeast in it, it doesn't rise or puff up into a loaf shape. It can be made very quickly because the baker doesn't have to wait for the dough to rise. Why do you think the Israelites only had time to make unleavened bread?** (They were in a hurry to escape from Egypt.)

2. **What else do you remember about the Israelites' escape from Egypt?** (God sent ten plagues to convince Pharaoh, the Egyptian ruler, to let the people leave.) **The name of this holiday, Passover, comes from the last plague. God had given the Israelites special instructions. They were to paint on their doorposts the blood of a lamb. On the night the Israelites escaped from Egypt, in any house that did not have the lamb's blood painted on its doorposts, the oldest son would die. Because death passed over the Israelite homes, the holiday is called Passover. The lamb killed at this celebration was called the Passover lamb. Jesus is called our Passover lamb because He gave His life to rescue us from sin.**

3. The Passover celebration helps people remember God's power. Read or ask an older child to read Exodus 12:24–27.

Conclusion

God's power helps us today too. Read Psalm 46:1 aloud. **What do you learn about God from this verse?** Pray, thanking God that we can depend on His power.

Discussion Questions

1. **When are some times kids your age need God's help?**

2. **When are some times God has helped you?** Tell your own answer before volunteers respond.

3. **What can we do to receive God's help?** (pray to God and ask for His help, read what God tells us to do in the Bible)

4. **Why can we depend on God's power and help?** (He loves us. He keeps His promises.)

Additional Information for Older Children

Yeast spreads through dough and causes the bread to rise or get bigger. **How does yeast remind us of sin?** (Each sin gets "bigger"—it causes other problems in the person's life.) **Throughout Scripture, yeast is compared to sin. Read 1 Corinthians 5:6–8 to find what the apostle Paul wrote about sin and how Jesus' death on the cross takes away our sin.**

Sending Portions
God's power helps us accomplish His plans.

Materials
- Bible with bookmarks at Esther 9 and Psalm 33:11
- basket
- canned foods *(optional)*

> **The plans of the LORD stand firm forever, the purposes of his heart through all generations.**
>
> Psalm 33:11

Introduction
God has many good things He wants us to do, and with His power He helps us to do them. Queen Esther, who lived long ago in Old Testament times, rescued her people to keep them safe as God had planned. Her brave and good actions are remembered with a special holiday called Purim (POO-rihm). Let's find out how this holiday is celebrated by Jewish people today.

Presentation
1. Display the basket you brought. **If you were to fill this basket with food for a friend, what would you put in it?** Accept responsess. Repeat the question, asking about gifts for a neighbor, a teacher, and a grandparent. *(Optional: Put canned foods in the basket to make a gift for a needy person.)* **Giving gifts to others, especially those in need, is one of the ways Purim is celebrated.**

2. **Purim is also celebrated by reading aloud the whole book of Esther. As the story is read, children in costumes act out the story of how God's people were saved. The audience cheers the good characters and boos the bad characters in the story. Purim is a day for celebrating God's power and doing good things to help others. The custom of giving gifts to friends and to the poor is written about in the book of Esther.** Read Esther 9:22 aloud. **This custom is called Mishloach Manot** (mish-LOCHE muh-NOHT). **In English *Mishloach Manot* means "sending portions."**

Conclusion
When we do things that show our love and obedience to God, we are following God's plans for us. Read Psalm 33:11 aloud. **This verse helps us learn that God's power is so strong that nothing can keep His plans from taking place. What are some of the good things God wants us to do?** (receive His love, become a member of God's family, talk to God in prayer) Pray, asking for God's help to do the good things He wants us to do.

Discussion Questions

1. **What did Esther and her people celebrate on Purim?** (Esther's brave actions, the defeat of Haman, God's power and care for them)

2. **What are some of the good things God has helped you do?** (be kind to a brother or sister, tell others about Him, help someone who was in danger)

3. **What are some ways to learn more of the good things God has planned for you to do?** (read God's commands in the Bible, ask teachers or older Christians, pray to God)

Additional Information for Older Children

The word *Purim* is the plural form of a Hebrew word that means "lots." The name refers to the way in which the evil Haman decided what day to destroy the Jews. Haman cast lots. That means to choose something by chance—like drawing straws or participating in a lottery. Another way in which Purim is celebrated is by eating a special pastry called hamantaschen. This pastry is shaped like a triangle to remind people of the shape of Haman's hat.

Thundering Sounds

Because God's power is greater than anything, He can help us when we're afraid.

Materials
- Bible with bookmarks at Psalm 29 and John 14:27
- picture of a storm, objects to make sound effects for rain and thunder—like a cookie sheet or drum (optional)

> **Peace I leave with you; my peace I give you.... Do not let your hearts be troubled and do not be afraid.**
>
> John 14:27

Introduction
When we're afraid, God can help us because His power is the greatest thing there is. Let's look at some of the ways we can see God's power in nature.

Presentation

1. **What kinds of sounds do you hear during a thunderstorm? How do you think we could make the sounds of a thunderstorm?** Accept responses. (Optional: Display picture of a storm.)

2. Children should suggest and practice sounds that can be used to represent a thunderstorm (rubbing palms together, snapping fingers, patting legs, stomping feet, etc.). After practicing sounds, divide the children into three groups and assign an order in which to make sounds. (Optional: Ask an older child to lead each group.) Direct the groups to make sounds as in a round. The first group begins a sound, followed in five to eight seconds by the second group and then the third group. When the first group begins a different sound, the other groups continue with the old sound until directed to change. (Optional: Have the children use objects to make sound effects for rain and thunder.)

3. **The sound of thunder is one way the Bible describes God's power.** Read or ask older children to read Psalm 29:3–4, 7 aloud. **These verses help us discover what God's power is like. How is the voice of God described in this psalm?** (majestic, powerful, like thunder and lightning) **God's power is greater than anything He has made.**

Conclusion

When have you been in a bad storm? How did you feel when you heard thunder? Let volunteers respond. Read John 14:27 aloud. **What does this verse tell us about being afraid?** (When we feel afraid, God promises to help us feel peaceful.) Pray, praising God for His great power and thanking Him for His help when we're afraid.

Discussion Questions

1. **What are some powerful things that kids your age might be afraid of?** (storms, earthquakes, tornadoes)

2. **Why can God help us when we are afraid of these things?** (He is the one true God. God created everything. He is more powerful than anything He created. He loves us and wants to help us.)

3. **How does God help us when we are afraid?** (He answers our prayers, gives us adults to help us feel safe, helps us remember His power, and gives us courage and peace.)

Additional Information for Older Children

Psalm 29 is a psalm of praise to God. This psalm has been called "The Psalm of the Seven Thunders" because it refers to the voice of God seven times. Many books of the Bible show God's power by comparing His voice to thunder. Have volunteers read the following Scriptures that compare God's voice to thunder: Job 37:5; Psalm 68:32–33; and Jeremiah 10:12–13.

Jesus

Balloon Pop

Because Jesus is alive, we know He will keep His promise to be with us now and forever.

Materials
- Bible with a bookmark at Matthew 28:20
- 2 large balloons
- clear tape
- sewing needle
- additional balloons *(optional)*

Preparation
Inflate (a little less than full) and tie the balloons. Place a 2" strip of tape on one the end of one balloon. Smooth over the tape to remove all air bubbles. Before class, practice step 2 below.

Introduction
All through our lives we need help—especially when things happen that make us afraid. Because Jesus is alive, He can protect and help us. Look at these balloons to find out what protects them.

Presentation
1. Hold up the needle and the balloon without the tape. **What will happen when I poke the balloon with the needle? The balloon doesn't have any protection against the sharp needle, so it will pop.** Use the needle to pop the balloon.

2. Hold up the second balloon. Firmly push the needle through the tape, keeping a good grasp on the needle. Then smoothly remove the needle. **Why didn't this balloon pop?** Accept ideas. **This balloon didn't pop when I poked it with the needle because it had something helping it to stay strong and not pop.** Show children the tape on the balloon. *(Optional: Depending on the number of children in your group and their ages, invite children to blow up balloons and attempt to pop them with and without tape.)*

Conclusion

Jesus promises to help us. Because Jesus is alive, we know He will keep His promises to us. Listen to Jesus' promise. Read Matthew 28:20 aloud. **Jesus promises to be with us now and forever, helping us and caring for us.** Lead children in prayer, thanking Jesus for His promise to be with us.

Discussion Questions

1. **When do people need to know of Jesus' help?**

2. **When are some times kids your age need to remember that Jesus is with them?**

3. **What are some other promises Jesus makes to His followers?** (to hear and answer their prayers, to forgive sins)

Believe It or Not
Believe Jesus is alive, and accept His love for you!

Materials
- Bible with bookmarks at John 3:16 and John 20:29
- bag containing objects for children to describe (unusual stuffed animal, kitchen utensil, tool, etc.)

Introduction
We accept Jesus' love for us and believe He is alive, even though we didn't see Him for ourselves! Let's try an experiment to discover why it sometimes might be hard to believe what other people tell us about something we didn't see for ourselves.

Presentation

1. Have several volunteers leave the room (or close their eyes). Show one of the objects and give the group several moments to look at it. When the volunteers return, describe the object to them, but don't use the words. (For example, for a stuffed animal don't say "stuffed" or "animal.") Volunteers return and try to guess what the object is based on children's descriptions. Repeat for each object you brought, reminding children not to use obvious words that would give away the object's identity.

2. **What made it difficult to figure out what the object was?** Accept responses. **Sometimes it's hard to believe something is true if you haven't seen it yourself. When Jesus rose from the dead, Thomas, one of His disciples, didn't believe Jesus was really alive because he hadn't seen Jesus with his own eyes. Even though we didn't see what Jesus did or hear what He said when He lived on earth—and even though we didn't see Him after He rose from the dead—we believe all these things happened. That's why we celebrate Easter! We can read God's Word that tells us exactly what the disciples saw and that they believed Jesus was alive! What did Jesus say about people who believe in Him without seeing Him?** Read John 20:29.

3. **Thinking about Jesus' death on the cross makes us feel sad, but it also helps us get ready to celebrate the exciting, good news of Easter Sunday when Jesus was alive again.** Ask children to demonstrate a face with happy and/or excited expression.

Conclusion

Because Jesus is alive, we can also have eternal life—life that lasts forever with God in heaven. Read John 3:16 aloud. Pray, thanking God that Jesus is alive and that He loves us.

Discussion Questions

1. **What are some of the things you believe about Jesus?** (He loves me. He forgives the wrong things I do. He makes it possible for me to be part of God's family.)

2. **Who has helped you learn to believe in Jesus?** (Sunday school teacher, parent, relative, friend)

3. **In what ways do kids your age show they believe Jesus is alive?** (pray to Him, obey His commands, read the Bible to learn more about Him)

Additional Information for Older Children

Jesus appeared several times to many different people in the days immediately following His resurrection. You can read about Jesus' appearance to two men traveling on the road to Emmaus in Luke 24:13–35.

Dead or Alive?
Jesus' death and resurrection were the fulfillment of God's promise of salvation.

Materials
- Bible with a bookmark at Romans 6:4
- 2 each of several examples of fruits with pits (avocados, peaches, olives, dates, plums)
- knife

Preparation
Before children arrive, cut open one of each kind of fruit and remove (but retain) the pits.

Introduction
All through the Old Testament, we read about God's promise to send a Savior. God kept His promise through Jesus' death and resurrection. Let's look at these reminders of how something that looks dead can grow new life.

Presentation
1. One at a time, show each fruit pit. **What fruit do you think this pit is from? Does the pit look dead or alive? Why? What would happen if this pit were planted in good soil and watered?**

2. Show each fruit. Invite children to match the fruit with the correct pit. After each fruit and pit are matched correctly, comment, **Even though the pits, or seeds, look like they are dead, new plants are able to grow from them.**

Conclusion
When Jesus died, His friends thought they would never see Him again. But God's power made Jesus come back to life again. Read Romans 6:4 aloud. **What does this verse say we may have because of Jesus' death and resurrection?** (a new life) **Jesus made it possible for us to become members of God's family.** Thank God in prayer for His gift of salvation.

Discussion Questions

1. **Why was Jesus the only one who could take the punishment for our sins?** (Jesus is the only person who never sinned. He is the one God promised to send.)

2. **When we choose to become members of God's family, what does He give us?** (forgiveness for our sins and eternal life)

3. **What are some other things in nature that remind us of new life?** (flowers, baby animals, butterflies)

Here's Jesus!

Jesus' baptism and John's announcement help everyone know Jesus is the Savior.

Materials
- Bible with a bookmark at John 1:29
- variety of newspaper and/or magazine ads and announcements (classified ad, product ad, store sale ad, upcoming event, etc.)

> **John saw Jesus coming toward him and said, "Look, the Lamb of God, who takes away the sin of the world!"**
>
> John 1:29

Introduction
In the Bible, the good news about Jesus was announced by John the Baptist. Today we hear about good news many of different ways. Look at these announcements to find what news is being told.

Presentation

1. One at a time show the ads and announcements you collected. Ask a volunteer to describe the message of each ad or announcement. **What are some other ways in which announcements are made?** (birth or graduation announcements, billboards, TV or radio commercials)

2. **All of these announcements tell things that will soon happen. But after a few weeks—after the sale is over or after the event has happened—we don't really need to remember the announcement anymore. The announcement John made about Jesus, however, is something people have always needed to know about and will remember for a long time! The words John said about Jesus are so important that everyone still needs to hear them.** Read John 1:29 aloud.

Conclusion
What kind of ad or billboard would you make to announce this good news about Jesus? Let volunteers share ideas. Lead the children in prayer, thanking God for the good news that Jesus is His Son.

Discussion Questions

1. **Why was Jesus called the "Lamb of God"?** ("Lamb of God" is a name for Jesus that tells us He died to take away our sins. Jewish people used to offer a lamb as a sacrifice to God for their sins; Jesus became like one of those lambs when He died.)

2. **What other news about Jesus would you like to announce to others?**

3. **How would you announce the good news about Jesus?**

Hidden Picture

We can worship Jesus as the Savior whom God sent for everyone in the world.

Materials
- Bible with a bookmark at John 8:12
- large picture of the wise men who visited baby Jesus
- large self-stick notes

Preparation
Completely cover the picture with rows of large self-stick notes.

Introduction
One of the best reasons to worship Jesus is because He is the Savior God sent for all the people of the world. In the Bible we read of some ways people found out about this good news. Let's find out who these people were and how they learned and celebrated the fact that Jesus is the Savior for everyone!

Presentation

1. Display the picture covered with notes. **What picture might be hidden behind these notes?** Invite one volunteer at a time to remove a note, asking each to guess what the picture is. Continue until all notes are removed.

2. **It's always exciting to discover something that has been hidden. A long time ago in Bible times, some men traveled a long way to discover a new King. Who were these men and who did they find?** (the wise men who found and worshipped Jesus) **The wise men were glad to have the Savior of the world shown to them** when they came to Bethlehem. This discovery of the wise men is celebrated around the world at a special holiday on January 6 called Epiphany. Epiphany comes from a Greek word that means "to show" or "to reveal."

Conclusion

Removing the notes helped you reveal and see what the picture was. The wise men helped show everyone in the whole world Jesus is God's Son and He came to be the Savior of everyone in the world! Read John 8:12 aloud. **When Jesus said He is the light of the world, He meant He shows people of all countries how to know God.** Pray, thanking Jesus for being the Savior of the world.

Discussion Questions

1. **What does it mean to worship Jesus?** (to show how much we love Him, to thank and praise Him)

2. **What can we thank Jesus for doing?** (loving us, hearing and answering our prayers)

3. **What are some other gifts we can give Jesus?** (bring an offering to church, obey Jesus and show His love by caring for others, thank Jesus when we pray)

Additional Information for Older Children

Matthew 2:1 tells us the wise men came from the east. Many Bible students believe they came from the area around Babylon. Years before, the Jewish people had lived as captives for 70 years in Babylon. One of these captives was Daniel, the Old Testament prophet. The wise men may have learned about the promise of the Messiah from the writings of Daniel. Read some of Daniel's writings about the Messiah in Daniel 7:13–14. Have the children find and read these verses.

Music Man

Knowing Jesus is God's Son and Jesus makes it possible for us to be part of God's family gives us joy.

Materials
- Bible with a bookmark at Psalm 95:1
- keyboard or other musical instrument
- recordings of Keith Green songs, music player *(optional)*

> **Come, let us sing for joy to the LORD; let us shout aloud to the Rock of our salvation.**
>
> Psalm 95:1

Introduction
We can have joy because we know Jesus is God's Son and He makes it possible for us to be part of God's family. Let's find out how one person was joyful because of what he knew about Jesus.

Presentation

1. Show and/or play the keyboard or other musical instrument. **What musical instrument do any of you play? How often do you practice your instrument? What do you like most about playing your instrument?** Let volunteers answer.

2. **Keith Green started playing instruments when he was only three years old. It didn't take him long to learn to play the piano and write songs. In fact, Keith's songs were recorded and sold when he was still a teenager. He loved music! When Keith grew up, he became a Christian. Knowing about Jesus' love made Keith so joyful he wanted to love and obey God and to tell everyone he could about Jesus. Keith and his wife, Melody, spent almost every night leading Bible studies for people who had no homes, drug addicts, and other people who needed help. But then, because of his love for God, Keith decided to write and sing songs to tell people about Jesus and how to follow Him. When Keith was 28 years old, he died in a plane crash. Many of the songs he wrote are still sung today because they tell the truth about what it means to love and obey Jesus.** *(Optional: Play one or more of Keith Green's songs.)* **It's sad to know Keith Green died, but as Christians we can have joy because we know that Keith is in heaven with a living Jesus.**

Conclusion
Read Psalm 95:1 aloud. **What are some ways Keith Green showed he felt joyful because of what he knew about Jesus?** Accept responses. **Let's thank God for Jesus.** Lead the group in prayer. Talk with interested children about becoming members of God's family (see "Leading a Child to Christ" on p. 8).

Discussion Questions

1. Psalm 95:1 tells us to "sing for joy to the LORD." When have you sung for joy? How is singing for joy different from singing because you have to?

2. What do you know about Jesus that makes you joyful?

3. What are some other ways to show we are joyful because Jesus is God's Son and makes it possible for us to be part of God's family?

Additional Information for Older Children

When Keith and Melody Green first became Christians, they lived in a small house. Many people came to their house to hear about Jesus and learn about Jesus' love for them. Pretty soon their small house was overflowing with people, and they were running out of space! So Keith and Melody bought the house next door, and when that house became too crowded, they rented five more houses on nearby streets!

Ready Wreaths

Get ready to celebrate the birth of the promised Savior.

> For to us a child is born, to us a son is given, and the government will be on his shoulders. And he will be called Wonderful Counselor, Mighty God, Everlasting Father, Prince of Peace.
>
> Isaiah 9:6

Materials

- Bible with a bookmark at Isaiah 9:6
- Advent wreath and candles
- matches
- picture of Advent wreath *(optional)*

Introduction

At this time of year, we're getting ready to celebrate the birthday of Jesus, the Savior sent by God. One word that describes this time of year means the same as "arrival" or "coming." Let's find out what this celebration is.

Presentation

1. **What are some ways your family gets ready to celebrate Jesus' birth?** Volunteers can answer. **A word that some people use when they talk about getting ready to celebrate Jesus' birth is the word** *Advent.* **Advent not only describes the season of the year in which we celebrate Jesus' birth, but it also describes four Sundays before Christmas when we can especially look forward or get ready to celebrate Christmas.**

2. Show the Advent wreath. *(Optional: Show the picture of the Advent wreath.)* **On the first Sunday of Advent, only the first candle is lit.** *(Optional: Light the candles as you describe them.)* **The first candle is called the Hope candle. It reminds us of Old Testament times when God's people hoped and waited for the Savior God had promised to send. On each of the following Sundays, another candle is lit. The second, or Peace candle, reminds us of the peace Jesus gives us. The third, or Joy candle, reminds us of the joy we feel at Jesus' birth. The fourth, or Love candle, reminds us of God's love for us and our love for God. Sometimes a fifth candle, called the Christ candle, is placed in the center of the Advent wreath. It is lit on Christmas Eve or Christmas Day to remind us of Jesus' birth.** *(Optional: As each candle is explained, invite volunteers to suggest a motion for the name of each candle. Ask children to describe other objects used at Advent—calendars, daily Advent candle, etc.)*

Conclusion

The prophet Isaiah looked forward to the coming of God's promised Savior. Listen to what Isaiah wrote. Read Isaiah 9:6 aloud. **This verse reminds us Jesus is the reason we celebrate!** Pray, thanking God for His love and for sending His Son, Jesus.

Discussion Questions

1. **Who was the promised Savior the Old Testament prophets told about?** (Jesus)

2. **What do you do to get ready for school? To go on a trip? To celebrate Christmas? What do you do that especially reminds you of Jesus' birth?**

3. **Because Jesus came to live on earth, what do we learn about God?** (God loves all people. God made a way for our sins to be forgiven.)

4. **Who has helped you learn about the coming of Jesus as our Savior?**

Additional Information for Older Children

What colors of candles have you seen in Advent wreaths? Invite responses. **Three purple candles are sometimes used in Advent wreaths to remind us of God's royalty. A pink or rose candle may be used for the Joy candle. The Christ candle is usually white and reminds us that Jesus is the light of the world. Advent not only celebrates Jesus' birth and the first time He came to earth, but it's also a time to look forward to His return!** *(Optional: Read Acts 1:9–11.)*

Washed Clean

Because God announced that Jesus is His Son, we can celebrate who Jesus is and become part of God's family.

> **The Son of God has come and has given us understanding, so that we may know him who is true.**
>
> 1 John 5:20

Materials

- Bible with a bookmark at 1 John 5:20
- objects used for baptism in your church
- dirty drinking glass, bowl of soapy water, towel, drinking water *(optional)*

Introduction

God announced that Jesus is His Son. When we believe Jesus is God's Son, we show we want to love and obey God with our actions. Let's look at some objects that remind us of one way of showing what we believe about Jesus.

Presentation

1. Display the objects that are used in your church for baptism. If children are familiar with these objects, invite volunteers to tell about them. Explain how each object is used and the baptismal method your church uses. *(Optional: Explain baptism in the following way: Show the dirty glass.* **Would you want to drink from this glass?** *Wash the glass and offer a volunteer a drink.* **We use water for cleaning. The Bible often compares washing with water to how God cleans the sin from our lives. Baptism is a special way to show that God washes us clean from sin and makes us ready to love and obey Him.***)* You may wish to invite your pastor or another church leader to come and explain the baptismal method used by your church.

2. **Jesus was baptized to show He was ready to completely obey God.** *(Optional: Ask a volunteer to read Matthew 3:13–17 aloud.)* **What are some ways we show love for God and obey Him?** (treat others in ways that please God, tell others about Jesus)

Conclusion

When Jesus was baptized, God was pleased and told the whole world Jesus was His Son. When we are baptized, we are telling the world we believe in Jesus as our Savior. Read 1 John 5:20 aloud. **This verse tells us we can get to know who Jesus is. What are some ways we can get to know Jesus?** (learn about Jesus at church, study God's Word, pray to Jesus) Pray, asking for God's help to know more about Jesus.

Discussion Questions

1. **God spoke from heaven to tell everyone that Jesus is His Son. What are some ways people make announcements today?** (by email or online, sending a letter or flier, telling the news on the radio or TV)

2. **What did Jesus do as God's Son?** (He died to save all people from their sins, healed people, cared for the sick and the poor, and taught people how to love others.)

3. **How can we help people today learn that Jesus is God's Son?** (invite them to church, tell them stories about Jesus)

Additional Information for Older Children

The Old Testament contains many prophecies about Jesus. The Old Testament prophet Isaiah wrote some words that describe the Savior God promised to send the world. Ask older children to find, read, and compare Isaiah 42:1 and Matthew 3:17. **The words God spoke at Jesus' baptism let everyone know that Jesus was the Savior written about in the Old Testament.**

Worldwide Praise

The birth of God's Son, Jesus, the Savior, is reason for the whole world to celebrate.

Materials
- Bible with a bookmark at 1 John 4:9
- nativity scene
- Christmas object from your cultural heritage *(optional)*

> **This is how God showed his love among us: He sent his one and only Son into the world that we might live through him.**
>
> 1 John 4:9

Introduction
The birth of God's Son, Jesus, is reason for everyone to celebrate. Many of our Christmas traditions, or the ways we celebrate Jesus' birth, actually began in other countries. Let's find out how one Christmas tradition began.

Presentation

1. **What do you know about the place where Jesus was born?** Invite responses. Display the nativity scene. **One of the objects we often see at Christmastime is a nativity scene like this one. People all over the world put up nativity scenes at Christmas to remind them of Jesus' birth.**

2. **Nativity scenes were first made in Italy about 800 years ago. Since then, people in countries all over the world make nativity scenes. In France, the nativity scene is used in place of a Christmas tree. In South America, a whole room is often decorated as a nativity scene, including drawings of hills, shepherds, the wise men crossing the desert, and even sailboats on the sea!** *(Optional: Show an object from your cultural heritage and explain its history and the customs surrounding it.)*

Conclusion
Nativity scenes are just one of the objects people all over the world use to celebrate the birth of God's Son, Jesus. Read 1 John 4:9 aloud. **What does this verse tell us is the reason God sent His Son to earth?** (God loves us.) Pray, thanking God for the gift of His Son, Jesus, and that we can celebrate Jesus' birth with people all over the world.

Discussion Questions

1. **Why should the whole world celebrate Jesus' birth?** (He came as the Savior for all people. God showed His love for the whole world when He sent Jesus.)

2. **What are some ways you've seen or heard the Christmas story?**

3. **What are some ways you, your family, or our church tell other people that Jesus has been born?**

4. **What are some ways we can help others celebrate Jesus' birth?** (send Christmas cards picturing events from the story of Jesus' birth, sing praise songs about Jesus)

Additional Information for Older Children

Most nativity scenes show the wise men worshipping Jesus at the stable. However, many people who study the Bible believe the wise men actually arrived in Bethlehem when Jesus was between one and two years old. There are two reasons for this belief. First, it probably took the wise men a while to research the meaning of the star they saw, to organize for their journey, and to travel a long distance. Second, when they arrived in Bethlehem, the Bible says they found Jesus in a house, not a stable. Read Matthew 2:11.

Worldwide Singing

We can celebrate with people all over the world the birth of God's Son, sent by God to keep His promise of a Savior.

Materials

- Bible with a bookmark at Luke 2:11
- world map or globe
- recording of "Silent Night" in a foreign language, music player, or guest singer *(optional)*

Introduction

The angels' message about Jesus' birth was such good news that people all over the world celebrate Jesus' birthday. Let's look at some of the places where people believe in Jesus and sing songs about His birth.

Presentation

1. Show the map or globe and point out the area where your church is located. *(Optional: Allow older children to find the locations.)*

2. Read Luke 2:11. **Another name for the town of David is Bethlehem.** Locate Bethlehem on the map or globe. **In the Old Testament part of the Bible, prophets told about God's promise to send His Son to be born in Bethlehem.**

3. **What are the names of some Christmas carols you remember?** Invite answers. **"Silent Night" is one of the most famous Christmas carols. This carol was first written in Germany.** Locate Germany on the map or globe. **A pastor of a church wrote a poem about Jesus' birth in Bethlehem. He gave the poem as a Christmas gift to his friend Franz Gruber. Later that same night, Mr. Gruber wrote a melody to go with the words. Everyone who heard the carol liked the words so much the carol spread all over the world.** *(Optional: Sing "Silent Night" together, play the recording of the carol in a foreign language, or ask someone to sing the carol in another language.)*

Conclusion

When we sing carols like "Silent Night," we can think about the thousands and thousands of people all over the world who sing this song in their own languages. Let's thank God for sending His Son to be born. Lead children in prayer.

Discussion Questions

1. **What are some of the ways people in our country celebrate Jesus' birth?**

2. **What are the ways people in other countries remember Jesus' birth?** (People in Mexico act out the story of Joseph and Mary looking for a place to stay. Christians in Israel plant seeds in front of nativity scenes; the growing seeds remind people of new life.)

3. **What is your favorite song to sing about Jesus' birth?**

Love for Others

A Ship in Danger

**Because we've experienced God's great love for us,
we can show compassion to others.**

Materials
- Bible with a bookmark at Luke 10:27
- toy boat or picture of a boat

> "Love the Lord your God with all your heart and with all your soul and with all your strength and with all your mind"; and, "Love your neighbor as yourself."
>
> Luke 10:27

Introduction
God's love and compassion for us are great! Because we know about God's love, we can show compassion to other people. Let's find out how someone showed compassion to people on a boat.

Presentation
1. Show the toy boat or picture of boat. **When have you sailed on a boat? What was the weather like?** Children can respond. **Sailing on a boat is fun when the weather is nice, but in cold and stormy weather, boats are dangerous places to be!**

2. **One cold winter day in a sea near the country of the Netherlands, the passengers on a boat were in big trouble. The weather was so cold the water was beginning to freeze. The boat was getting stuck, and the people couldn't get to shore. To make matters worse, the rescue crew from the nearest city would not help the passengers on the boat because the passengers were all members of a church the rescue crew hated. The passengers were stranded at sea! But one man, Menno Simons, heard about the passengers on the boat. Menno belonged to a different church. Menno and some of his friends from his church decided to help the stranded passengers. Menno and his friends risked their lives in the icy water and rescued all the passengers!**

Conclusion
Read Luke 10:27 aloud. **What is another way to describe how this verse says we are to love God?** (We are to love God with everything we have and in every way we can.) **How did Menno Simons and his friends obey Luke 10:27?** Lead children in prayer, thanking God for His love and asking Him to help children show His love to others.

Discussion Questions

1. **What does it mean to show compassion to others?** (to care about others and do what you can to help them)

2. **How has God shown compassion to us?** (He sent Jesus so that we could be forgiven. He promised to help us and be with us.)

3. **When is a time you can show compassion to someone in your family? To your friends? To someone at school?**

Additional Information for Older Children

Many government leaders in the country of the Netherlands didn't like Menno Simons and the other members of his church. They wanted to stop people from becoming members of Menno's church. The government leaders thought if they could stop Menno from telling others about God, they could stop his church from growing. They offered a reward of 100 gold coins to anyone who would tell them where Menno was. But God protected Menno. No one ever turned him in to collect the reward!

Balloon Drop
Loving God means loving all kinds of people.

Materials
- Bible with a bookmark at Ephesians 4:2
- balloons
- balls *(optional)*

> **Be completely humble and gentle; be patient, bearing with one another in love.**
>
> Ephesians 4:2

Introduction
The Bible is full of stories about what it means to love God. One way to love God is to show His love to all kinds of people by caring about their needs. Let's watch someone in our group try to help another person.

Presentation
1. Invite a volunteer to stand next to you. **Let's see how many balloons** _____ (name of child) **can hold.** Ask other children to blow up the balloons and give them to this volunteer to hold. *(Optional: To save time, blow up the balloons beforehand or use balls instead of balloons.)*

2. When the volunteer cannot hold any more balloons, ask him or her to help you with a task (open or shut a door, find verse in Bible, etc.). After the volunteer expresses difficulty in helping you while still holding onto the balloons, ask, **What would you have to do in order to help me?** (drop the balloons) **When others need our help, sometimes we need to drop what we're doing or put aside until later something we're doing so we can help them.**

Conclusion
Listen to Ephesians 4:2 to find the word that describes someone who thinks about what others need instead of always thinking about oneself. Read Ephesians 4:2 aloud. **Someone who is humble cares about other people and wants to help them. What else does this verse say we should do?** (be patient with others as a way of showing love) **Ephesians 4:2 doesn't say to care only about people we like or who like us. When we say we love God, it means we want to show His love to all kinds of people.** Lead the children in prayer, asking God's help in showing love for Him by caring for others.

Discussion Questions

1. **In what way has someone been patient with you? Helped you with something you needed?**

2. **When might you need to stop doing something in order to help someone who needs help?** (stop watching TV when a parent needs help setting the table, stop playing a game at recess when a friend gets hurt)

3. **When might it be hard to do what Jesus wants you to do? What can we do when we need help loving and obeying Jesus?**

Birthdays around the World

God created us as unique people who can know Him and love one another.

Know that the LORD is God. It is he who made us, and we are his."

Psalm 100:3

Materials
- Bible with a bookmark at Psalm 100:3
- objects used to celebrate birthdays (choose from those listed below)

Introduction
God created all the people in the world so we would know Him and love one another. One way we show love to others is by celebrating their birthdays. Let's look at some ways birthdays are celebrated around the world!

Presentation

1. **What do you like to do to celebrate your birthday?** Volunteers can share. **Birthdays are good times to show love to people and to celebrate the unique ways in which God made them.**

2. Display and discuss the objects you brought that are associated with some of the following birthday traditions: China—friends and relatives join in a lunch of noodles to wish the birthday child a long life; Denmark—a flag is flown outside a window to show that someone in the house is having a birthday; Japan—the birthday child wears all new clothes; Mexico—the birthday child uses a bat to break open a piñata, which is stuffed with candy and small toys to be shared; Philippines— blinking lights decorate the home of the birthday child; Russia—the birthday child receives a birthday pie with a greeting carved in the crust; United States—the birthday child receives a birthday cake with one candle for each year of the child's age. *(Optional: Children can reenact one or more of the traditions.)*

Conclusion
Read Psalm 100:3 aloud. **According to this verse, to whom do we belong? Why?** (God because He made us) **God created us and wants us to know and love Him. God also wants us to show His love to others. No matter what the tradition, birthdays are a time to celebrate and show love to people we care about.** Pray, thanking God for creating us and asking His help in loving each other.

Discussion Questions

1. **How did God show His love in the ways we are created?** (He made our bodies in amazing ways and gave us minds to think.)

2. **What are some ways we can get to know God?** (read the Bible; listen to older people who love God talk about Him; ask your parents, pastor, or teacher questions about God)

3. **Why should we show love to other people?** (Doing so shows God's love. Jesus tells us loving God and loving others are the most important things to do.)

4. **What are some ways to show love to other people?** (be kind to them, help them with tasks they are doing, care for them when they are upset, be patient with people who sometimes annoy you)

Additional Information for Older Children

The most important birthday ever was the day Jesus Christ was born. How did the shepherds celebrate the birth of the baby Jesus? Let volunteers answer or read Luke 2:16–20. **Who else came to celebrate the birth of Jesus?** (the wise men) **How did they worship Jesus?** Children can tell about the gifts given by the wise men or read Matthew 2:9–11.

Circle Attraction

Giving to others doesn't depend on our wealth because Jesus helps us give more than money.

Materials
- Bible with a bookmark at Ephesians 5:2
- hole punch
- tissue paper
- small round balloon
- extra balloons and tissue paper *(optional)*

Preparation
Use the hole punch to make 20 to 30 little tissue-paper circles. Inflate and tie the balloon.

Introduction
Jesus helps us give more than money to others. Our gifts of love can make a big difference. Watch the different actions that take place in this experiment.

Presentation

1. Place the tissue-paper circles on a table.

2. Rub the balloon against your hair (or carpet) at least ten times. Then hold the rubbed side of the balloon several inches above the paper circles. The paper circles will be attracted to the balloon and jump off the table onto the balloon.

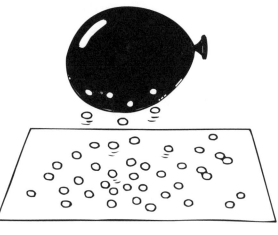

3. As time permits, invite volunteers to take turns creating the attraction between the balloon and the paper circles.
(Optional: Provide additional balloons and circles so that multiple volunteers can participate at once.)
Rubbing the balloon makes an electric charge that attracts, or pulls, the paper circles.

Conclusion

When we show Jesus' love to others, it attracts them to Jesus and helps them want to learn about Jesus. Read Ephesians 5:2. **How does this verse describe the way Jesus' followers should live? What should we be like?** Volunteers can tell their ideas. Lead the children in prayer, asking for God's help in giving and showing love to others.

Discussion Questions

1. **What other kinds of things attract each other?** (Magnets attract many metal items. Flowers attract bees. Gravity attracts, or pulls, falling objects.)

2. **How does showing Jesus' love help others learn about Him?** (helps others discover what the people who love Jesus are like, helps them understand how much Jesus loves them)

3. **How has someone shown Jesus' love to you and your family?**

4. **How can you show Jesus' love to someone else?**

Double Trouble

We can show God's love through attitudes and words that are gentle and respectful.

Materials
- Bible with bookmark at 2 Timothy 2:24–25
- photograph of a newborn or young baby

Introduction

Our gentle and respectful words and attitudes show God's love to others. Let's find out about a woman who was gentle and respectful, even though she didn't agree with what others were doing.

Presentation

1. Show the photograph of a baby. **How do people usually treat a newborn or young baby?** Let children respond. **Many years ago, people in a village in Africa felt afraid when they saw babies who were twins. These people believed that twin babies were evil and should be killed. The people wouldn't even walk on a road on which a mother of twins had walked!**

2. **In 1876 a woman named Mary Slessor lived near this village. Mary wanted to help the people there learn about God's love. One day, Mary heard that twins had been born in the village. Mary quickly ran through the jungle to the village, hoping to save the lives of the babies. When Mary arrived, one of the babies was already dead, but the other one was alive. Mary gently took the baby and started walking back with the baby's mother to Mary's house. As she was walking on the road, however, Mary realized that if the mother walked on the road, the people wouldn't walk on that road again. They would have to work hard to cut a new road through the jungle. So instead of ignoring the people's beliefs, Mary showed respect for the people and had a path cut through the jungle straight to her house. Mary took care of the baby, and soon many people in the village learned to love the baby too. And best of all, because of Mary's gentle actions, the people kept coming to her house and learned about God's love for them!**

Conclusion

Read 2 Timothy 2:24–25 aloud. **People who love God are sometimes called servants. How did Mary Slessor show that she was God's servant?** (She was gentle and kind and helped others learn about Jesus.) **Let's ask God to help us remember to use words and attitudes that are gentle and respectful.** Lead the children in prayer.

Discussion Questions

1. **When has someone treated you gently and respectfully? What did that person do? What did you do?**

2. **Why do you think God wants us to treat others gently and respectfully?** (because He loves all people)

3. **What are some gentle and kind words you like to hear?** ("Thank you," "Sorry," "You can have the first turn," words that are encouraging instead of bossy, words that show we care about the other person) **When is it hard to use kind and gentle words?**

Additional Information for Older Children

One time when Mary Slessor needed to build a new building to use in teaching people in the village about God, she asked the chief of the village for help. Though the chief agreed to send people to help her, several days passed and no one showed up. Instead of yelling and complaining, Mary simply started doing the work herself! Mary chose to be gentle and kind, even when it was hard.

Love Songs
The fruit of the Spirit is shown through our love for God and others.

> **Over all these virtues put on love, which binds them all together in perfect unity.**
>
> Colossians 3:14

Materials
- Bible with a bookmark at Colossians 3:14
- copy of the hymns "Take My Life, and Let It Be" and "Who Is on the Lord's Side?" by Frances Havergal *(optional)*

Introduction
The fruit of the Spirit is shown through our love for God and others. Let's learn how one woman showed her love for God through her whole life!

Presentation
1. Hold out your hand. **What do you use your hands to do?** Repeat the question, substituting feet and voice. **Frances Havergal is a woman who wrote a song about how she wanted to use her hands, her mouth, her money—her whole life! Frances said she wanted to use everything in her life to show her love for God and obedience to Him. She even wrote a poem about that, and it became a famous song.** *(Optional: Read the words of "Take My Life, and Let It Be" or sing the hymn together.)*

2. **The words Frances wrote were not just nice-sounding words to her. She actually gave away most of her money to help others. And she often studied the Bible. In fact, Frances memorized the entire New Testament and several books in the Old Testament. Frances spent her whole life loving God. She started writing poems about her love for God when she was only seven years old. Before she would do anything or write any songs or poems, Frances would pray. In fact, the words of "Take My Life, and Let It Be" are a prayer to God. Frances only lived to be 42 years old, but she wrote many books and poems, including more than 60 songs that still help people tell about their love for God.**

Conclusion
Read Colossians 3:14 aloud. **What does this verse say we are to "put on" or show? How did Frances Havergal show her love for God?** (She memorized portions of the Bible. She prayed. She wrote poems and songs about God.) Lead the children in a prayer to express their love for God. *(Optional: Read or sing the hymn as a prayer.)* **A great way to show our love for God is to become members of His family.** Talk with interested children about becoming members of God's family (see "Leading a Child to Christ" on p. 8).

Discussion Questions

1. **How can you show love for God with your hands? Your feet? Your voice?**

2. **What are some actions that show love for God?** (singing songs of praise to God, telling others about Jesus, praying, helping someone in need, obeying God's commands, giving an offering)

3. **What are some actions that show love for others?** (helping someone who is hurt, being honest, saying kind words)

4. **What is a way you can show love for God this week? Show love for others?**

Additional Information for Older Children

One of the songs Frances wrote is "Who Is on the Lord's Side?" The title for this song is taken from Exodus 32:26, when Moses asks God's people to choose if they will love and obey God. Ask a volunteer to read the verse aloud. Then ask a volunteer to read the words of the first stanza of the song "Who Is on the Lord's Side?" **How did Frances describe what it means to be on the Lord's side? How might kids your age show that they want to love and obey God?**

Music of Courage
God can give us courage to love our enemies.

Materials

- Bible with bookmarks at Psalm 57:8; 150:3–6; and Luke 6:27
- variety of musical instruments (tambourine, cymbals, guitar, autoharp, keyboard, rhythm instruments, etc.)
- guest musician with instrument, music from your collection, music player *(optional)*

Introduction

If we pray and ask, God gives us courage to show love to our enemies. In Bible times, people often sang and played instruments to pray for courage or other things. Let's find out about some of the instruments they used.

Presentation

1. Read or ask an older child to read Psalm 150:3–6 while other children count the number of instruments mentioned. **Lyres are like small harps. The way instruments sound often helps us express the feelings of the words we are saying or singing. What kind of feeling would a cymbal make you think of?** Accept responses.

2. **Psalm 57 is a song written by David at a time when he needed God's courage to love his enemy Saul.** Read Psalm 57:8 aloud. **David talked about harps and waking up in the morning. What instruments would remind you of waking up?** Volunteers can answer.

3. Distribute the instruments to volunteers. **Use these instruments or your hands to make sounds for other phrases in Psalm 57: people chasing someone** (see v. 3), **lions or spears and arrows** (see v. 4), **people falling in a pit** (see v. 6), **a heart constantly beating** (see v. 7). Children can experiment with making different sounds. *(Optional: Invite a musician to make sounds on an instrument such as an electric guitar or synthesizer.)* **At the end of this psalm, David praised God for His love.** *(Optional: Play a song for children to accompany with instruments.)*

Conclusion

David was able to show God's love even when Saul didn't deserve it. Read Luke 6:27 aloud. **God has promised that He will give us the courage to do what is right. All we have to do is ask.** Pray, thanking God for His love and asking Him for courage to love everyone, even our enemies.

Discussion Questions

1. **What are some ways to show love, and do good things for people you might think of as enemies?** (don't be mean back to them, don't say mean things about them to others, smile and be friendly to them)

2. **In what ways can we obey Luke 6:27?** (be kind to others who are mean to us, pray for people who don't like us, be kind even when others aren't)

3. **What can you do when it seems too hard to show God's love to an enemy?** (ask God for courage to do what's right, ask a parent or teacher for advice on how to show love)

Additional Information for Older Children

Psalm 57 is one of a group of psalms that relate to the history of Israel. Psalms 42–72 are about the great deeds God has done for His people, especially those recorded in the book of Exodus. (Optional: Children can look up and read Psalm 44:1 and 47:1–3 aloud.)

Prison Reform

We can follow Jesus' example of showing love to people others might ignore.

Materials
- Bible with a bookmark at John 15:12
- bag containing 6–8 school supplies (pencil, notebook, eraser, ruler, pencil sharpener, crayons, folder, book, etc.)

Introduction
Jesus showed love to people who other people ignored. Let's find out how one person followed Jesus' example and how we can follow His example too.

Presentation

1. Show the bag. **This bag is full of things you might need for school.** Invite volunteers to guess what items are in the bag. Show items that the children correctly guess, and then identify any items not guessed. **A long time ago in England, some children didn't have any of these things. They didn't even have a school to go to, because they lived with their mothers in prison. The children hadn't done anything wrong; but at that time, children had to go to prison with their mothers if they didn't have other family members to care for them.**

2. **Even though most people didn't care about prisoners, a woman named Elizabeth Fry visited this prison. She was shocked by the horrible conditions in which the women and their children lived. Within a few years, Elizabeth helped to organize a school for the children and collected the school supplies they needed. Then she set up a room where the women prisoners could learn to sew. Elizabeth also wanted the prisoners to know about Jesus' love for them. She talked about Jesus to the women and children and read from her Bible about Jesus' love and forgiveness. Elizabeth's work to help women and children in prison became so well-known that people in the English government and even the queen of England, Queen Victoria, gave money to support her work.**

Conclusion
Read John 15:12 aloud. **How did Elizabeth Fry obey this verse?** Accept responses. **Let's thank God for Jesus' example and ask Him to help us show His love to others.** Lead the children in prayer.

Discussion Questions

1. When have you felt ignored? How did another person help you?

2. Who are some people kids your age often ignore or don't pay any attention to? (younger children, kids they don't like)

3. What are some things you could do to care for someone who doesn't seem to have any friends?

Additional Information for Older Children

Elizabeth Fry made sure the women prisoners were given Bibles and other things they needed. Many of her ideas for helping women who were in prison became laws in England and other countries. Elizabeth became very famous for her good works. In addition to helping women in prisons, Elizabeth taught children to read in Sunday school, helped start libraries, and even started a school to train nurses in caring for people.

Salt Surprise

Keep telling about God your whole life, looking for ways in every situation to share God's love with others.

Materials

- Bible with a bookmark at 1 Peter 3:15
- plastic wrap
- bowl
- tape
- salt
- measuring spoon
- metal pan with a lid

> **Always be prepared to give an answer to everyone who asks you to give the reason for the hope that you have.**
>
> 1 Peter 3:15

Preparation

Tightly stretch a piece of plastic wrap over the bowl, taping it securely. Practice step 1 below to make sure the plastic wrap is tight enough.

Introduction

It's important for God's followers to keep telling others about Him, giving reasons why we believe in and love God. See if you can figure out the reason or explanation for why something in this experiment moves without anyone touching it.

Presentation

1. Sprinkle one teaspoon of salt evenly onto the plastic wrap. Then invite a volunteer to stand several feet from the bowl and bang the lid onto the pan at the level of the top of the bowl. The salt will move on the plastic wrap.

2. As time permits, invite additional volunteers to take a turn banging the pan. Ask volunteers to tell reasons why they think the salt moves. Acknowledge each child's idea.

3. **We've talked about some ideas about why the salt moves. Listen to the reason or explanation according to scientists: we can't see sounds, but they are vibrations in the air, so sounds make the air move. These vibrations in the air make the plastic wrap move or vibrate so that the salt moves.**

Conclusion

Hearing a reason for why something is true helps us understand it better. Listen to 1 Peter 3:15 to find what God wants us to be ready to give a reason for. Read the verse aloud. **The hope we have is our belief in God and His love and forgiveness for us. This verse reminds us to tell others about what we believe.** Lead the children in prayer, asking His help in telling others about His love.

Discussion Questions

1. **What do you know about God that others should know? About Jesus?**

2. **Who has told you about Jesus and helped you learn about reasons to love and obey Him?**

3. **What are things kids your age can do to learn about Jesus?** (read the Bible, listen to stories from the Bible, ask parents or teachers to help you understand what verses from the Bible mean)

Love from God

Circle Talk

Because Jesus is alive, we know He will keep His promise to be with us now and forever.

Accept one another, then, just as Christ accepted you, in order to bring praise to God.

Romans 15:7

Materials

- Bible with a bookmark at Romans 15:7
- large sheets of paper or whiteboard
- markers

Introduction

It's important to remember God's love is for everyone. Let's find out what some of the people who God loves are like.

Presentation

Write the names of two volunteers above the circles. Then interview those two children to find several differences and similarities between them, writing the similarities in the overlapping area of the circles and writing the differences in the separate areas of the circles. **What do you like to do at school? What is your favorite TV show? Favorite color? Favorite food? What color are your eyes?** As you fill out the diagram, talk about the ways children are the same and different. God made people alike in some ways and different in others. Continue the activity with other volunteers and new circles.

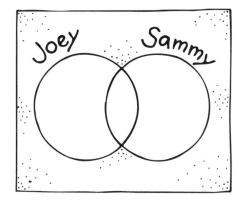

Small Group Option

Group children into pairs. Give each pair a Venn diagram and invite them to draw pictures or write words to show their differences and similarities.

Conclusion

Listen to Romans 15:7 to find out what God wants us to do for each other if we are alike or different. Read the verse aloud. **When we accept others, it means we want to show God's love by telling them the good news about Jesus and treating them in kind and fair ways. God's love is for everyone.** Write "Loved by God" in the overlapping area of all the circles. Pray, thanking God for His love and asking His help in showing love to others.

Discussion Questions

1. How are you alike or different from the people in your family? A friend in your neighborhood or class at school?

2. How do you think you might be alike or different from a kid your age who lives in a country far away from here?

3. **How might you help someone who is different from you learn about God's love? How might you accept that person and treat him or her fairly?** (invite him or her to go to church or the park, speak up when others are picking on him or her)

Gifts of Love
The greatest love is God's love for us!

Materials
- Bible with bookmarks at John 15:13 and 1 Corinthians 13:4
- 8½" x 11" sheet of paper
- scissors
- markers
- variety of Valentine's Day gifts (heart-shaped candy box, valentine cards, flowers, etc.) in a large bag

Preparation
Make a pop-up card. Fold and cut the paper (see sketch a). Keeping the card closed, fold as shown (sketch b). Open the card, draw and cut a heart, and draw a cross (see sketch c). Fold the top portion of the heart down inside the card at an angle. Decorate the front of the card to resemble a valentine.

Introduction
The greatest love in all the world is God's love for us! Valentine's Day is a day to thank God for His love and show love to others. Let's look at some of the ways people tell others they are loved.

Presentation

1. **What kinds of things do people give each other on Valentine's Day?** As children suggest gifts, display examples from the Valentine's Day gifts you brought.

2. **On Valentine's Day we give cards and gifts to tell people we love them. But the best, the greatest, gift of love ever given was not given on Valentine's Day.** Open the pop-up card you prepared. **What gift does this card remind you of?** (God's gift of salvation through Jesus) **When was it given?** Let volunteers respond. **God's gift of His Son, Jesus, is the greatest gift of love ever given.** Read or ask an older child to read John 15:13 aloud.

Conclusion
Listen to this verse that tells what we can do to show God's love to others. Read 1 Corinthians 13:4. **What are the ways to show love this verse names?** (being patient, being kind) **What are some ways you can show patience and kindness this week?** (wait for someone else to share, help someone who is hurt) Pray, thanking God for His great love and His greatest gift, Jesus.

Discussion Questions

1. **Why is God's love the greatest love of all?** (He always loves us, no matter what. He is always patient and kind toward us. We may forget to love people all the time, but God always loves us.)

2. **How does God show His love for us?** (He sent Jesus to teach people about God and to die on the cross for our sins. God cared for people since the world began. He hears and answers our prayers. He gives us families and friends to love us.)

3. **What words would you use to describe God's love to someone else?** (huge, the greatest, faithful, patient, kind)

4. **What are some ways we can show God's love to others?**

Additional Information for Older Children

There are several stories about the man Valentine's Day was named after. According to tradition, around AD 270 a man named Valentine was put in prison because he worshipped God. While in prison, he continued to show love for God by helping others. Because of his faith, Valentine was killed. After his death, leaders in the church began a feast, or holiday, to help members of God's family remember God's love.

Honorable Mention
You are important to God!

Materials
- Bible with bookmarks at Matthew 19:14–15 and 1 John 3:1
- objects used to recognize deserving people (trophy, blue ribbon, certificate, award, etc.)
- guest to pray a blessing *(optional)*

> **See what great love the Father has lavished on us, that we should be called children of God!**
> 1 John 3:1

Preparation
Place the objects around the room. *(Optional: Arrange to have a pastor or other church leader say a prayer of blessing for the children.)*

Introduction
Each of you is important to God! Let's talk about some of the ways we show we think people are important.

Presentation

1. **What are some awards or honors you've received? Contests you've won?** Let volunteers respond. **When people win contests or are given awards, we find ways to let them know what they did was important.** Ask volunteers to search for and identify the objects you placed around the room.

2. **Many times today people are honored because they have done something special. But Jesus didn't honor children because they had done something special. Jesus loves all children. Jesus made sure the disciples knew that children were important to Him when He showed how glad He was to see them.** Read Matthew 19:14–15. **Jesus recognized how important children are. Today many countries, schools, and other organizations set aside special days on which to honor children and show how important they are.**

3. **Some churches have a Sunday on which children are honored. On this day, a special prayer or blessing is said for each child. When we bless someone, it means we ask God to do good things for the person.** *(Optional: A pastor or other church leader says a blessing for the children.)*

Conclusion
Read 1 John 3:1 aloud. **When we are members of God's family, we know we are loved by God and are important to Him.** Pray, thanking God for His love and asking Him to show His care and protection to each child in the group.

Discussion Questions

1. **How are important people usually treated?** (given a red carpet, given a special seat, get driven around in a special car, have people to help them do everything)

2. **How do we know we are important to God?** (The Bible tells us. We are called His children.)

3. **What things does God do to show that you are important to Him?** (He listens to and answers my prayers. He sent Jesus to take the punishment for my sins so I can live forever with God. He gives me people who love and care for me.)

Additional Information for Older Children

Many countries—including Japan, Australia, and Turkey—have national holidays in honor of children. In Turkey on Children's Day, children switch places with government leaders. The president, prime minister, the cabinet minister, and city and state leaders turn over their jobs to children who even sign laws into effect!

Memory Lane
God's actions show His love for us.

Materials
- Bible with a bookmark at Psalm 105
- baby book or photo album of baby pictures
- paper, pencils, markers *(optional)*

> **Sing to him, sing praise to him; tell of all his wonderful acts.**
>
> Psalm 105:2

Introduction
God shows His love for us through His actions. Often, we make memory books or photo albums showing the actions of other people. Let's look at an example of a memory book and find out how we can remember God's loving actions.

Presentation

1. **How many of you know the name of the city where you were born? How old you were when you first walked? The day your first tooth came in?** Invite responses. Display the baby book or photo album. **This is a special book some parents put together to help them remember the actions of their children when they were babies.** Describe some of the contents of the baby book or photo album.

2. **In Old Testament times, God's people wanted to remember the loving actions of God. So when the people gathered together to celebrate special occasions, one of the priests would read special songs to remind the people of all the amazing things God had done for them.** Read or ask an older child to read Psalm 105:1–5. **Psalm 105 describes some of the wonderful things God did for Abraham, Jacob, Joseph, Moses, and all the Israelites! These reminders of God's loving care gave the Israelites good reason to celebrate!** *(Optional: Children can write or draw their own reminders of things God has done for them and their families.)*

Conclusion
Read Psalm 105:2 aloud. **What are some of the things God has done for you or your family?** Volunteers can respond. **As we remember all the good things God has done for us, we have reason to celebrate too!** Pray, thanking God for His love and all the great things He has done for us, remembering things mentioned by volunteers.

Discussion Questions

1. **When is a time a kid your age might experience God's loving care?** (when He answers prayer, when He provides food)

2. **What are some good ways to learn more about God's loving acts?** (read the Bible, ask older people who love God about His great acts)

3. **What has God done for you or people you know to show His love?** (He has given us families to care for us, houses to be warm in, and people to tell about Him.)

4. **What can you do to tell others about God's loving acts?**

Additional Information for Older Children

Many psalms were written by David to praise God. Often we can find out what was happening in David's life at the time he wrote a particular psalm. Find Psalm 105:1–15 and 1 Chronicles 16:8–22 in your Bibles. Compare the verses in these passages. Have the children read the passages and describe similarities and differences. Then ask a child to read 1 Chronicles 16:1 to find the event for which David wrote these words.

Missionaries of Charity
Our kind actions demonstrate God's love.

> As God's chosen people, holy and dearly loved, clothe yourselves with compassion, kindness, humility, gentleness and patience.
>
> Colossians 3:12

Materials
- Bible with a bookmark at Colossians 3:12
- objects with slogans (T-shirt, bumper sticker, poster, ads, etc.)
- photo of Mother Teresa *(optional)*

Introduction
Our kind actions demonstrate God's love. Let's learn about a woman whose kind actions helped people around the world experience God's love.

Presentation

1. Show the objects and ask volunteers to read the slogans aloud. **When people want others to know important things they believe, they often write slogans.**

2. **In 1910 a special girl was born in the Republic of Macedonia, a country in Eastern Europe. During her teenage years, this girl joined a group of young people who raised money for the poor and learned about missionaries in foreign lands. The motto of this group was "What have I done for Christ? What am I doing for Christ? What will I do for Christ?" This motto showed how important these** teenagers thought it was to love and obey Jesus. **When this young lady was 18, she decided to serve Christ by becoming a missionary in India. For the rest of her life, she lived among the poorest people in India. She taught street children and comforted the sick and dying. She became known as Mother Teresa. Other women joined her, forming a group called the Missionaries of Charity.** *Charity* **is another word for love. Today this group has more than 500 centers around the world where the hungry, the sick, and the dying are cared for.** *(Optional: Show the photo of Mother Teresa.)*

Conclusion
Read Colossians 3:12 aloud. **How did Mother Teresa obey this verse?** Accept responses. Lead the children in prayer, asking for God's help serving those who are in need so that others can learn more about God's love.

Discussion Questions

1. **What are some ways people have shown kindness to you or someone you know?**

2. **What are some kind actions you can do at home? At school? In your neighborhood?** (let a brother or sister choose which video to watch, help parents empty the dishwasher, invite a new kid to play a game at school, carry groceries for a neighbor)

3. **Why do your kind actions help other people learn about God's love?** (They can see some of the ways God cares for them.)

4. **What is one kind action you can do this week? For whom?**

Additional Information for Older Children

The Missionaries of Charity spend their time cleaning people's bloody wounds, feeding dying people, and rocking abandoned babies. When one missionary was asked if she got tired of doing this difficult work, she said she could never get tired because she loves and cares for each person as if the person was Jesus himself (see Matthew 25:40).

Never-Ending Love
God keeps His promises to show His faithfulness.

Materials
- Bible with a bookmark at Psalm 117:2
- 2 strips of paper 12" x 2"
- scissors
- tape
- extra paper strips and scissors *(optional)*

> **Great is his love toward us, and the faithfulness of the LORD endures forever.**
>
> Psalm 117:2

Introduction
God's love and His faithfulness last forever. Something that lasts forever has no end. Let's make something that doesn't have an end or a beginning—and gets bigger and bigger.

Presentation
1. Hold up the two strips of paper. **Where's the beginning of these strips? The end?**

2. Tape the strips together at one end to make one long strip. Flip one end of the strip over (see sketch a) and tape it to the other end, so paper loop has a twist. Make sure the joined ends are completely covered with tape.

3. Fold the strip and cut the middle of the loop (see sketch b). The loop will expand to double the size of the original. Cut the middle of the loops at least one more time.

Small Group Option
Prepare two strips for each child to tape together. The children will then cut the loop at your direction.

Conclusion

Now our paper strips have become a big loop that has no beginning or end. **What does Psalm 117:2 say lasts forever?** Read Psalm 117:2 aloud. **Faithfulness means always keeping your promises and doing what you say you will do. God is faithful, and His promises last forever.** Thank God for keeping His promises.

Discussion Questions

1. **What are some things other than God's love and faithfulness that don't seem to have a beginning or end?** (sky, ocean)

2. **What are some of God's promises to us?** (He always hears our prayers, always helps us, and never leaves us.)

3. **When might someone your age need to remember one of these promises?**

Overflowing Love

God's gift of the Holy Spirit made it possible for the family of believers to grow as they showed God's love and care.

> **God's love has been poured out into our hearts through the Holy Spirit, who has been given to us.**
>
> Romans 5:5

Materials
- Bible with a bookmark at Romans 5:5
- small glass jar
- large baking pan with sides
- measuring utensils
- baking soda
- vinegar
- food coloring

Introduction
The Holy Spirit is God at work in our lives and in the world. God's gift of the Holy Spirit makes it possible for His followers to show love and care for others. When we accept God's love, it overflows to others. Watch to see what overflows in this experiment.

Presentation

1. Set the jar in the middle of the baking pan. Pour one tablespoon of baking soda into the jar. Measure one cup of vinegar and add several drops of food coloring to the cup. Pour the vinegar into the jar. The liquid will bubble up and overflow the jar.

2. **When the vinegar and baking soda were mixed together, they formed a gas called carbon dioxide. The gas pushed the liquid out the top of the jar so the liquid overflowed.**

Conclusion
The Bible talks about how God's love can overflow. Read Romans 5:5 aloud. **God loves us so much He wants each of us to show His love to others. God showed His love to us by sending the Holy Spirit. The Holy Spirit helps us show love to others so that the family of people who believe in God can grow.** Lead the children in prayer, thanking God for sending the Holy Spirit and asking His help in showing His love to others.

Discussion Questions

1. **What are some other things you have seen that overflow?** (a river or lake that overflows its banks, a soda can that has been shaken before opening) **God made all these things that overflow.**

2. **What are some of the other ways God has shown His love to us?**

3. **What are some ways we can show God's love to others?**

4. **How has someone shown God's love to you?**

Ties of Love

God shows His love through the actions of people He gives to care for us.

Materials

• Bible with bookmarks at Ephesians 6:1–3 and 1 John 4:11
• variety of neckties
• 1 or more medals *(optional)*

Introduction

Through the actions of the people God gives to care for us, we can see His love. Let's find out about something we can give to honor people who care for us.

Presentation

1. *(Optional: Show one or more medals)* **What kinds of things do people receive medals for?** (winning a game or contest, courageous action in rescuing someone) **Some medals are called badges of honor.** Display the neckties you brought. **A necktie might also be thought of as a badge of honor. In 1660 King Louis XIV of France saw brightly colored silk handkerchiefs around the necks of some war heroes from a country called the Republic of Croatia. He decided to make silk neckwear a sign of royalty. Over time, men everywhere started wearing ties.**

2. **Who do you know who wears neckties? When are some times you might give a necktie as a gift? Many people give their fathers and other important men in their lives neckties on Father's Day. The next time you give someone a necktie, remember that you are giving a badge of honor for all the ways that this person cares for you!** *(Optional: Distribute the neckties to children and allow them to experiment with tying them around their own necks.)*

3. Read Ephesians 6:1–3 aloud. **What does this verse say is the right thing to do?** (obey parents, honor parents) **God gave us fathers and other people to love us and take care of us. Who loves and cares for you? What might you give that person to honor him or her?** Let volunteers respond.

Conclusion

God loves us so much He gives us fathers and other people to take care of us. Read 1 John 4:11. **What are some ways you can show love to others? By showing love to others, we are showing our love for God! Loving and caring for others is one of the best ways we can show God's love.** Pray, thanking God for all the people He gives to care for us. Ask for His help in showing love to others.

Discussion Questions

1. How does knowing God gives us people who care for us make you feel? Why do you think God wants us to have people who care for us?

2. What are some ways fathers care for their children? Who cares for you in this way?

3. How can you thank people who care for you? Why do you think these people want to care for you?

Additional Information for Older Children

When we say the word *father*, we are usually talking about our parents. In the Bible, instead of referring only to parents, the word *father* is also used as a title of respect for rulers, elders, and priests. Have the children find and read Scriptures about men who were called father as a way of showing respect for them: Joseph—Genesis 45:8; Elijah—2 Kings 2:11–12; Elisha—2 Kings 13:14.

What Do You Need?

No matter what we need, God helps and cares for us.

Materials
- Bible with a bookmark at Philippians 4:19
- picture or photo of a baby (or a baby doll)
- apple
- sharp object

> **My God will meet all your needs according to the riches of his glory in Christ Jesus.**
>
> Philippians 4:19

Introduction
No matter how young or old we are and no matter what we need, God says He will give us what we need. Sometimes it seems like we don't get the things we need. Let's talk about why we might feel that way and discover if it's really true.

Presentation
1. Show the picture or photo of a baby or pass around the doll, letting volunteers pantomime ways of caring for a baby. **What are some of the ways people care for babies? How do babies get the things they need? Someone who cares for a baby will make sure to give the baby things like food, water, milk, hugs, and toys to play with.**

2. **Listen to this verse about the things we need.** Read Philippians 4:19. **What does this verse say God does?** (God gives us the good things we need.)

3. **The Bible tells us to ask God for the things we need. But sometimes we ask God for something but we don't get it. Because God loves us so much, He might say no to our request because He knows what we've asked for isn't good for us.** Show the sharp object, keeping it out of the children's reach. **If a baby wants to play with a _____** (name of object)**, how do people protect the baby?**

4. **Other times when we ask God for something, His answer is to wait.** Show the apple. **Why is an apple good for you to eat? Why is an apple not good for a baby to eat?** (A baby might choke on apple pieces.) **Just as babies have to wait until they are older to eat apples, God knows we have to wait for some things.**

Conclusion
When we pray and ask God to give us the things we need, we know His answers are always best. Lead the group in prayer, thanking God for meeting our needs.

Discussion Questions

1. **What are some of the things God provides for us?** (people to care for us, food to eat, friends to play with)

2. **How do people show they are depending on God to give them what they need?** (ask God for needs, don't complain about things they want but don't have)

3. **What's something you are thankful God has given to you?**

Obeying God

A Chance to Learn

Don't miss an opportunity to show goodness by doing what is right.

> As we have opportunity, let us do good to all people, especially to those who belong to the family of believers.
>
> Galatians 6:10

Materials

- Bible with a bookmark at Galatians 6:10
- item typically given to a teacher as a gift (bell, apple, sign saying "Thank you, teacher!" etc.)

Introduction

We should use every chance we have to show goodness by doing what is right. Let's find out about someone who showed goodness and helped others because she did what was right.

Presentation

1. Hold up the teacher gift. **Have you ever given something like this to one of your teachers or seen anything like this on one of your teachers' desks? What other kinds of gifts might make a teacher feel special?** Volunteers can respond. **A long time ago, a teacher named Prudence Crandall got the opposite of a thank-you gift from the people who lived around her school.**

2. **In the early 1800s, when people were still fighting about slavery, Prudence Crandall started a school for teenage girls in Connecticut. All the girls attending the school were white. At that time, some people did not want to be friends with African Americans. So when Prudence welcomed an African American girl to attend the school, the people in her town became angry. They took their daughters out of the school. But Prudence loved all of God's people and wanted to give African American students a chance to learn. She invited more African American girls to the school to take the place of the students who had left. Now the townspeople became very upset! When a group of angry townspeople attacked her school, Prudence closed the school because she was afraid the girls would get hurt. It seemed like anger and hatred had won. But when some of her students grew up, they helped other African American girls get an education. The good choices Prudence Crandall made caused many people to be able to learn. That was even better than receiving a thank-you gift!**

Conclusion

Read Galatians 6:10 aloud. **What does this verse tell us to do for all people? How did Prudence Crandall do good for others?** (She tried to help young girls by teaching them, even though other people didn't want her to.) Close in prayer, thanking God for the opportunity to do good and asking for His help in choosing to do what is right.

Discussion Questions

1. **When might a kid your age be able to show goodness by choosing to do what is right?** (choosing to say something nice to a kid who is being teased, letting your brother or sister have the first turn instead of fighting about whose turn it is)

2. **When has someone shown goodness to you by doing what was right? How did that make you feel?** Tell your own answer as well as asking volunteers to respond.

3. **What are some ways to learn the right things to do?** (read the Bible, listen to parents or teachers, watch older people who love Jesus)

Additional Information for Older Children

Prudence Crandall was arrested and put on trial because of her efforts to help young African American girls. Even though Prudence was found guilty and had to spend time in jail, her trial ended up helping others. More than 100 years later, some of the things said at her trial were used in the Supreme Court of the United States to make new laws that help African Americans get good educations.

Direction Signals

Loving and obeying God your whole life are the wisest things to do.

Materials
- Bible with bookmarks at Psalm 62 and Mark 12:30
- music from your collection
- music player

Introduction
Loving God and obeying His directions our whole lives are the wisest things we can do. Let's look at some ways people are directed to do things.

Presentation

1. Ask children to identify various hand directions or signals. For instance, place your index finger in front of your puckered lips. **What am I directing you to do when I do this?** (be quiet) Continue with hand directions that mean "come here," "go away," "stop," "time out," and so on. *(Optional: Ask volunteers to suggest and demonstrate hand directions.)*

2. **Another time when hand directions are used is when a director is leading a band or a choir.** Ask a volunteer to read the phrases written under the Psalm 62 heading in the Bible: "For the director of music. For Jeduthun. A psalm of David." **Who wrote the psalm?** (David) **Who is Jeduthun?** (the director of music) **This psalm was written for the director of music, Jeduthun, to use when he directed the songs of praise to God during worship services.**

3. Lead the children in singing the song you've selected. Divide the children into two groups. Ask a volunteer to alternately point to each group. Only the group being pointed at sings. The volunteer may also use hand signals to direct each group in singing loudly or softly.

Conclusion
Read Mark 12:30 aloud. **What are the four ways we are directed to love God?** Volunteers can respond. **The more we love God, the more we want to obey Him. And that's the wisest thing we can do!** Pray, asking God for His help to love Him and obey His directions every day.

Discussion Questions

1. **Why are loving and obeying God our whole lives the wisest things we can do?** (God tells us the best ways to live. We avoid making mistakes when we do things the way God tells us to.)

2. **Name some Bible people who showed they loved and obeyed God by their actions. What are some of those actions?**

3. **What can you do to show that you love and obey God?** (praise Him with songs, pray to God telling Him why you love Him, obey God's commands in the Bible, tell the truth, care for others)

Additional Information for Older Children

The Hebrew word *selah* (SEE-lah) occurs twice in Psalm 62 (just in a footnote in some Bibles) as well as in many other psalms. No one really knows what *selah* means! Some people believe it is a musical direction that tells when the musicians should play loudly in between the phrases of the song. Other people think *selah* indicates when a pause in the singing should take place. Read Psalm 4 where the word *selah* appears and decide which definition you think is correct. Guide children to find and read the verses, and then discuss the usage of the word *selah*.

Emergency Kit
God helps us do what's right, even when it's hard.

Materials
- large bag with these objects inside: Bible with a bookmark at Psalm 119:66, eraser, a framed photo of a friend and/or family member

> **Teach me knowledge and good judgment, for I trust your commands.**
> Psalm 119:66

Introduction
A first-aid or emergency kit usually has bandages and medicine in it. I have a bag that is like an emergency kit for people who love God. Let's find out what's in the bag.

Presentation

1. Show the bag to the children and shake it slightly so children hear the objects inside. Invite one or more volunteers to feel the outside of the bag and try to guess what the objects might be.

2. As you take each item out of the bag one at a time, explain how the object reminds us of what it means to do what's right. **This eraser reminds us of making mistakes. Obeying God doesn't mean we'll never make mistakes. God erases our wrong actions by forgiving our sins when we ask Him to. This picture of a friend reminds us that God gives us moms and dads, grandmas and grandpas, sisters and brothers, and friends who will pray for us and help us know what God wants us to do.**

Conclusion
The best part of obeying God is that God gives us the Bible to help us obey Him. Read Psalm 119:66 aloud. **To have good judgment means to be wise and know the right things to do and say. We know that we can depend on God to help us be wise and make good choices.** Ask God's help in doing what's right.

Discussion Questions

1. **What promises in God's Word do you remember? What instructions?** Tell an example of a promise or instruction that has helped you obey God. Older children may find and read a promise or two: Joshua 1:9; Psalm 23:1; Proverbs 3:5–6.

2. **Who is someone God has given you to help you learn what God wants you to do?**

Eyes of Faith
Our right actions can help others do what is good.

Materials
- Bible with a bookmark at 1 Timothy 4:12
- old eyeglasses or sunglasses with petroleum jelly smeared on the lenses

> **Don't let anyone look down on you because you are young, but set an example for the believers in speech, in conduct, in love, in faith and in purity.**
>
> 1 Timothy 4:12

Introduction
The good things we do and the right choices we make can help other people do good things too. Let's find out how someone who couldn't see very well was an example to many people.

Presentation

1. Have volunteers try on the glasses you prepared. **What are some things it would be hard to do if this is how you could see?** Let children tell their ideas. **A woman named Henrietta Mears had very poor eyesight, but that didn't stop her from doing great things.**

2. **When Henrietta Mears was a child, her doctor said that she would probably become blind. So as she grew up, Henrietta decided to study hard, read a lot, and memorize large portions of the Bible in case she later lost her eyesight. Henrietta's eyes were a problem for her throughout her life, but the doctor's prediction never did come true. She was never completely blind. When Henrietta grew up, she became a high school teacher in a small town. She was determined to help her students learn to do good things. When Henrietta discovered that her school didn't have a football team, she hired a coach and helped organize the team. Henrietta went to every game to cheer for her students. Soon the football players started coming to Henrietta's Sunday school class, where she taught them about the Bible. By the end of one year, many young people had decided to believe in Jesus and had learned to love and obey God because of Henrietta's teaching.**

Conclusion

Read 1 Timothy 4:12 aloud. **How was Henrietta Mears an example to others?** Children can tell their ideas. **Let's ask God to help us do what is right so other people can learn about Him.** Lead the children in prayer. **Jesus is the best example any of. us can follow. Because of what Jesus did for us, we can become members of God's family.** Talk with interested children about becoming members of God's family (see "Leading a Child to Christ" on p. 8).

Discussion Questions

1. **Whose good example have you followed? Who might follow your good example?** (younger brother or sister, friend, someone at school) How?

2. **What kinds of good actions might happen in a living room? In a kitchen? In a bedroom?** (helping a child with his or her homework, clearing the dishes from the table, reading a story to a younger brother or sister at bedtime, sharing the computer)

3. **How might our right actions help another family member do good?** (Reading a story to a younger brother might help him fall asleep. Clearing a table might help a parent have time to call a lonely friend.)

Additional Information for Older Children

Henrietta Mears was an example to many well-known Christian leaders, including Billy Graham. Henrietta started a publishing company to produce Sunday school curriculum. She also started a Christian camp many children and adults attend every year. Her poor eyesight did not stop her from doing good!

Growing in Obedience
When we know God's Word, it shows in our lives.

Materials
- Bible with a bookmark at Psalm 119:11
- samples of different grains (barley, rice, rye, corn, rolled oats, wheat, wheat germ, cracked wheat flour, muesli cereal, puffed oat or rice cereal, etc.)

> **I have hidden your word in my heart that I might not sin against you.**
>
> Psalm 119:11

Introduction
When we know God's Word, it shows in our lives by the good decisions we make and the right actions we take. One of the ways people in Bible times celebrated the Feast (or Festival) of Weeks was by bringing offerings of grains they had grown and harvested. Let's discover how these growing things remind us of obeying God's Word.

Presentation

1. Show samples of different grains, passing the samples around to the children and allowing them to taste if desired. (Check for allergies.) **Where do all these kinds of food come from?** (They are grown. You can make bread or cereal from them.) **These are grains. Unlike fruits or vegetables that also grow from the ground, grains are the seeds of plants, mostly different types of grass.**

2. **At the Feast (or Festival) of Weeks, also called Shavuot** (shah-voo-OHT), **the Hebrew word for "weeks," God's people celebrated and thanked God for the good things that grow from the earth. When we plant a seed and care for it by giving it light and water, the seed grows and produces grain. When we read and think about God's Word, it grows and produces good things in our lives. What are some of the good things that can grow out of our lives by studying God's Word?** (courage to be honest, kind ways to treat others, patience, knowledge to make good choices)

Conclusion
When we read God's Word and follow what it says, God helps us live the very best way. Read Psalm 119:11 aloud. **According to this verse, what should we do to keep from sinning? What do you think it means to hide God's Word in our hearts?** (Read God's Word and remember it.) **One important thing God's Word tells us about is how to become members of God's family.** Talk with the children about becoming Christians (see "Leading a Child to Christ" on p. 8). Pray, thanking God for His Word and asking for His help in obeying it.

Discussion Questions

1. **When might kids your age read and think about God's Word?** (when hearing a Bible story at church, when reading a Bible story with parents)

2. **Who has helped you learn from God's Word?** (parents, grandparents, teachers)

3. **What do we learn from reading God's Word?** (how to love and obey God, how to show His love to others, how to become members of God's family)

Additional Information for Older Children

The Feast of Weeks took place at the end of the barley harvest. Because the first sheaf of the barley harvest was to be dedicated or given to the Lord, the first day of the Feast of Weeks is called Firstfruits. Read Leviticus 23:9–10 aloud. **Until the dedication was made, no bread, grain, or anything from the harvest could be eaten! The people wanted to give God the first and best part of their harvest.**

Making Friends
Patiently continue to do what is right in all situations.

Materials
- Bible with a bookmark at 1 Corinthians 15:58
- bucket
- rope
- small prize for each child

> **Stand firm. Let nothing move you. Always give yourselves fully to the work of the Lord.**
> 1 Corinthians 15:58

Preparation
Tie the rope onto the bucket's handle. Place the prizes in the bucket.

Introduction
Doing what's right, even in difficult situations, is a way to show patience. Let's find out how a man showed patience in a hard situation.

Presentation
1. **What kind of gift would you give a friend? Volunteers can respond. I'm going to give you a gift in an unusual way today.** Hold the bucket by the rope and invite each child to take a prize from the bucket. **Usually when people exchange gifts, it shows that they are friends. Let's find out how a man named Jim Elliot gave gifts in a bucket to try to make friends with some dangerous people.**

2. **Jim Elliot and four other missionaries lived in the country of Ecuador in South America. The missionaries wanted to tell a group of people called the Aucas (OW-kuhs) about Jesus. But there was a BIG problem. The Aucas were not friendly people. In fact, they usually killed anyone who came near their villages! But the missionaries didn't give up. First, they patiently learned how to say words in the Aucan language. Then for several months, they flew over the Aucas' villages, lowering buckets filled with gifts for the Aucas. As they lowered the buckets, they called out greetings to the people. Even in this hard situation, Jim Elliot patiently kept trying to make friends with the Aucas. Eventually, the missionaries were able to meet the Aucas face-to-face.**

Conclusion
Read 1 Corinthians 15:58. **"Stand firm" means you should keep doing what is right and trust in God. What is one way Jim Elliot and his friends stood firm and did the work of the Lord?** (They continued to try to make friends with the Aucas, even though it was hard.) Pray, asking God to help the children patiently do what is right.

Discussion Questions

1. **What are some situations in which it is hard to have patience and do what is right?** (when your brother or sister keeps bothering you, when someone is yelling at you, when you are tired and don't want to do what is right)

2. **What is one right action you can take when, for example, your younger brother keeps taking your markers?** Repeat the question, substituting other situations in which patience might be needed.

3. **What is "the work of the Lord"?** (loving others, obeying God's commands)

4. **Name one time at school when it is hard to do what is right. How can you patiently keep doing right in that situation?** Repeat the question, substituting other times, places, or situations for the phrase "at school."

Additional Information for Older Children

Shortly after Jim Elliot and his friends met the Aucas, they were killed by the Aucas. Some people thought all of Jim's efforts to make friends had been wasted. But several years later, Jim's wife and another woman became friends with the Aucas and lived in their village. Because the missionaries patiently kept doing what was right, many Aucas became Christians.

Rainbow Fun
People who love God obey Him.

Materials
- Bible with a bookmark at John 14:15
- 6 glasses
- measuring cup
- light corn syrup
- glycerin (found in most pharmacies)
- water
- cooking oil
- rubbing alcohol
- red, yellow, green, and blue food coloring
- 4 spoons

If you love me, keep my commands.

John 14:15

Introduction
God's instructions help us know the best way to live.
Watch what happens when I follow these instructions.

Presentation
Read the directions aloud as you complete each step. Or have an older child read aloud as you work.

1. Set out the glasses and pour a half cup of each liquid into separate glasses in the following order: light corn syrup, glycerin, water, cooking oil, rubbing alcohol.

2. Using separate spoons, stir several drops of food coloring into the liquids: red into light corn syrup, yellow into glycerin, green into water, none into cooking oil, blue into alcohol.

3. Pour about 1" of each liquid into the remaining glass as follows: (A) pour red into the center of the glass without letting liquid hit the side; (B) tilt the glass and pour yellow into the point where red meets the side of the glass (see sketch a); (C) pour green liquid down the side of the tilted glass; then clear; then blue. Each liquid should float on the top of the previous liquid. Hold the glass upright to see the rainbow (see sketch b).

Conclusion
Following these directions helped me make a rainbow. Following God's directions or commands is even better! They help us know the best way to live. Read John 14:15 aloud. **Because I love. God, I want to obey Him.** Ask God's help in obeying.

Discussion Questions

1. **What would have happened if I hadn't followed the directions?**

2. **Being honest is a direction or command God wants us to obey. What are some of the results of being honest?** (parents and friends trust you and like to be with you, teachers know they can depend on you)

3. **What are some ways you can show love for God and obey His commands?** (be honest, care about the needs of others)

Running the Race

We show goodness by choosing to obey God, even when it is hard.

Materials
- Bible with a bookmark at Acts 5:29
- a sports medal or trophy

We must obey God rather than human beings!

Acts 5:29

Introduction
We show goodness by choosing to obey God. Let's find out about one man who chose to obey God, even when it was hard.

Presentation
1. Show the sports medal or trophy. **How do you think I got this award?** Let volunteers guess where the item came from. **Many athletes dream of the chance to win Olympic medals.**

2. **Eric Liddell** (lih-DEHL) **was an athlete in England who could run very fast! In 1924 he hoped to win a gold medal at the Olympics. But when the race schedules were announced, Eric discovered he was supposed to run in a race on a Sunday. Years before, Eric had said he would not work or play sports on Sundays. He made this choice to show his love and obedience to God. Eric wanted to spend time worshipping God on Sundays not running races. So Eric said he would not run in the Sunday race. When people in England heard about Eric's decision, they were furious! They thought Eric didn't care about his country. But Eric started training for a different race that did not take place on Sunday. No one thought he could win this race, however, because it was longer. On the day of the race, much to everyone's surprise, Eric not only won the race and the gold medal, but he also ran this race faster than anyone else in the world had ever run it!**

Conclusion
Read Acts 5:29 aloud. **How did Eric Liddell show that he wanted to obey God? Why might it have been hard for him to show goodness in this way?** Accept responses. Pray, asking God to help the children choose to obey Him, even when it is hard.

Discussion Questions

1. **How do we know what God wants us to do?** (by reading what He tells us in the Bible, by listening to our parents) **What are some things God's Word tells us to do?** Volunteers can respond. Invite older children to read one or more of the following passages aloud: Exodus 20:12; Galatians 5:14; 1 Thessalonians 5:16–18; James 1:19; 1 John 3:11.

2. **Why is it most important to obey God?** (His laws are the best, even when they are hard. He loves us. He is God, the maker of everything. God's laws tell us how to follow His plans.)

3. **When are some times it is hard to obey God's commands?** (when you feel tired or angry, when you don't know God's commands, when everyone else is disobeying God's commands) **Why do you think it's important to obey God, even in those hard times?**

4. **Name one way you can show goodness by obeying God's commands this week.**

Additional Information for Older Children

Throughout his life, Eric Liddell made choices that showed goodness. Just one year after winning the Olympic gold medal, Eric went to the country of China as a missionary. For 20 years, Eric Liddell helped people in China learn about Jesus. The story of Eric Liddell's life and his good choices was told in the movie *Chariots of Fire*.

Talk Radio

Being careful in what you say shows self-control.

Materials
- Bible with a bookmark at James 1:19
- books from the Chronicles of Narnia series by C. S. Lewis
- Lewis's book Letters to Children (optional)

> **Everyone should be quick to listen, slow to speak and slow to become angry.**
>
> James 1:19

Introduction
One way to show self-control is to be careful about what you say. Let's find out how one man was careful about what he said.

Presentation

1. Show the books you brought. **The Chronicles of Narnia is a series of books written by a man named C. S. Lewis. What do you know about these books?** Volunteers can tell what stories they know. **C. S. Lewis wrote these books to help children learn about loving and obeying God. But Mr. Lewis also did many other things in his life.**

2. **Clive Staples Lewis was born in Ireland in 1898. He joined the army to fight for England during World War I and was a brave army officer. But during World War II, C. S. Lewis helped people in another way in England. During the war, while the Nazis were bombing cities in England, many people listened to C. S. Lewis talk on the radio about what it meant to be a Christian. C. S. Lewis carefully chose what to say so all kinds of people could understand God's love for them, even when bad things—like a war—happened. The talks helped people see that loving and obeying God was the most important thing to do. So many people were helped by the radio talks that some of the talks were later written down in a book called** *Mere Christianity*. **Even today people learn about being part of God's family from this book.**

Conclusion
Read James 1:19 aloud. **Being "slow to speak" means being careful about what you say. How did C. S. Lewis show he was careful in the things he said?** (When talking on the radio, he was careful about what he said so that all kinds of people could learn about God.) **When we listen to others and are careful about what we say, we show self-control. Let's ask God to help us listen to each other and use self-control in what we say.** Lead the children in prayer.

Discussion Questions

1. **When might it be hard to show self-control when you talk to others?** (when angry or upset, when someone says something unkind)

2. **When are some times it might be difficult for kids your age to listen?** (when they're tired, when they're hungry, when someone is taking a long time to speak)

3. **What can you do that will help you listen better and control what you say?** (follow James 1:19 and be "quick to listen" and "slow to speak," pray and ask God for His help, count to ten before speaking if upset, walk away before saying something that shouldn't be said)

4. **What should we do when we make mistakes and say things we shouldn't?** (ask for God's forgiveness and apologize to the people we were talking to)

Additional Information for Older Children

Many people wrote letters to C. S. Lewis, including children who had read the Chronicles of Narnia. He spent a lot of time answering these letters. Some of the letters he wrote back to these children were published in a book called *Letters to Children*. Invite children to tell what they would write in letters to C. S. Lewis. *(Optional: Read aloud some of the letters from Letters to Children.)*

Worldwide Travel

Show God's goodness by making sure your words and actions match.

Materials
- Bible with a bookmark at 1 John 3:18
- world map
- information about Samaritan's Purse *(optional)*

> **Let us not love with words or speech but with actions and in truth.**
>
> 1 John 3:18

Introduction
We can show God's goodness by making sure our words and actions match. Let's find out about a man who became known for loving and obeying God with both his words and actions.

Presentation

1. Show the world map. Invite a volunteer to point out the country in which you live. **What other countries have you traveled to or heard of?** Volunteers can name countries and locate those countries on the map. Give help as needed. **Today we are going to talk about a man named Billy Graham. He traveled to more than 185 countries!**

2. **In 1934 Billy Graham went to a church meeting and heard a preacher talk about Jesus. Because of what he learned about Jesus at that meeting, Billy decided to love and serve God for his whole life. So after Billy went to college, he started telling people about Jesus' love and how to become a member of God's family. Billy not only told people about Jesus' love, but his actions also showed Jesus' love. Billy traveled to cities all over the world to preach about Jesus. He talked to people who were kings and to people who were members of tribes in Africa. He preached in huge football stadiums and in small villages. Every place Billy preached, many people decided to become members of God's family. Everyone who met Billy saw that both his actions and words showed Jesus' love.**

Conclusion
Read 1 John 3:18 aloud. **Billy Graham's words and actions showed he obeyed this verse. Who are some other people you know who love God and others with their actions as well as with their words?** Volunteers can briefly tell about people they know. **Let's ask God to help us show goodness by making sure our words and actions match.** Lead the children in prayer. **Billy Graham used his words to help other people become members of God's family.** Talk with interested children about becoming members of God's family (see "Leading a Child to Christ" on p. 8).

Discussion Questions

1. **Why is it important for what you do to match what you say you believe?** (Our actions show what we really believe. Our good actions can help others do what is good.)

2. **When are some times it might be hard for a kid your age to act in ways that show goodness? How could you help a friend in a situation like this?**

3. **Making our words match our actions is one way to show goodness. How does God help us have the fruit of goodness?** (He gives the Bible to help us understand right ways to act, reminds us of ways to speak and act to show goodness, and answers our prayers for help.)

Additional Information for Older Children

Billy Graham's son, Franklin Graham, also traveled and preached about God. Franklin Graham also became the leader of Samaritan's Purse, a group of people who help people all over the world. For many years at Christmastime, Samaritan's Purse has collected shoe boxes of gifts that are given to poor children in many countries. *(Optional: Find additional information at www.samaritanspurse.org.)*

Peace

A Dangerous Journey

We can ask God for wisdom to settle arguments and live in peace with others.

> **Let us therefore make every effort to do what leads to peace.**
>
> Romans 14:19

Materials
- Bible with a bookmark at Romans 14:19
- sheriff's badge
- construction paper, marker, scissors, straight pin *(optional)*

Preparation
Make a badge from construction paper (see sketch; *optional*)

Introduction
God will help us live in peace with others when we ask Him for help and wisdom to settle arguments. Let's find out about a man who had to be very brave to live in peace.

Presentation
1. Invite a volunteer to wear the sheriff's badge. **What is the job of someone who wears a badge like this?** (sheriff, police officer) **How does a sheriff or police officer keep the peace?**

2. **In the 1800s a young man named Samuel Morris had a chance to help others live in peace. Samuel was sailing on a ship from the African country of the Republic of Liberia to America, because he wanted to go to school to learn more about God. The sailors on the ship, however, didn't like Samuel because he was African. One angry sailor even threatened to kill him! One day, that sailor thought others were making fun of him, so he swung his sword to attack them. Samuel jumped in the way, putting his own life in danger, and shouted, "Don't kill!" The angry sailor surprised everyone by putting down his sword and walking away. Everyone was amazed! After that, whenever there was a fight, Samuel helped to stop it and kept the peace by praying for the men. Samuel Morris showed he was willing to do whatever he could to help people live peacefully together.**

Conclusion

Read Romans 14:19 aloud. **What does it mean to "make every effort"?** (try as hard as you can, to do something to the best of your ability) **How did Samuel Morris show that he made every effort for peace?** (Even though he could have been hurt or killed, he stopped the sailor with the sword from hurting anyone.) Invite volunteers to pray, asking God to help them do actions that will help friends and family members live in peace.

Discussion Questions

1. **When have you been a peacemaker or settled an argument while playing with friends? With your family?** First, tell children an age-appropriate example about God giving you wisdom to be a peacemaker. Second, ask volunteers to share their stories.

2. **When is one of the hardest times for you to remember to be a peacemaker?**

3. **How can you make every effort to do what leads to peace at home? At school?** (let a brother or sister be first or borrow something when he or she asks, ask God for wisdom about how to treat a classmate who is being mean, don't argue, don't tease)

Additional Information for Older Children

Samuel Morris was born a prince in Africa. When he was a teenager, he was taken prisoner when his people lost a battle. Samuel was tortured when his father could not pay the ransom. After sailing to America, Samuel attended Taylor University in America for only one year before he died from injuries he had received when he was tortured. But during that year, Samuel helped many people learn to trust and obey God. Many people at Taylor University decided to become missionaries because of Samuel's actions.

Fair Pay for All
Putting others first can help us be peacemakers.

Materials
- Bible with a bookmark at Romans 12:18
- Help Wanted section of newspaper or print one from an online newspaper

> **If it is possible, as far as it depends on you, live at peace with everyone.**
>
> Romans 12:18

Introduction
Every day we have opportunities to help others live in peace. Peacemakers do what they can to put the needs and interests of others first. Let's find out what one man did to be a peacemaker.

Presentation

1. Show the Help Wanted section of the newspaper. **What do people use this part of the newspaper for? Why might finding a job be hard?** Children can share their ideas. **There are all kinds of reasons people might have a hard time finding jobs. Some people have had trouble finding good jobs just because of the color of their skin.**

2. **John Perkins was an African American who had a hard time finding a job for fair pay. He once worked for a farmer all day and received only 15 cents as payment! Because of problems like these, many African American people believed they needed to fight to be treated fairly.**

3. **When John Perkins grew up, he became a Christian. He wanted to help African Americans be treated fairly without fighting. So John started telling people in Mississippi about Jesus. Sometimes he was yelled at and even beaten, but he still worked hard to help African Americans get fair pay. One time a friend of John's told him about a man and woman who were so poor they didn't have any food or a place to live. John said he would help the man and woman. When they came for help, however, John was surprised to see they were not African American! John wondered if he should help them or not. But he soon realized that because God loves everyone the same, white people deserved help from him too. John's hard work helped people of all races get good jobs and fair pay.**

Conclusion

Read Romans 12:18 aloud. **What does the verse mean when it says we should live at peace with others "as far as it depends on" us?** (It means we should not start fights or arguments. It means we should try to end arguments or fights, instead of continuing them.) **In what ways was John Perkins a peacemaker?** (He helped others to get good jobs and fair pay without fighting.) Lead the children in prayer, asking God to help them do what they can this week to live at peace with others.

Discussion Questions

1. **When might a kid your age need help to live in peace with others?** (when someone says something mean, when someone cheats in a game)

2. **Who are some peacemakers you know?** (police officers, people who break up fights, people who walk away from arguments)

3. **What can you do to make peace if someone wants to quarrel?** (stop a fight instead of continuing it, ask an adult for help, pray and ask God for courage to be a peacemaker)

Additional Information for Older Children

John Perkins started the Harambee (HAR-ahm-bay) **Christian Family Center in Pasadena, California. The word** *Harambee* **is Swahili and means "let's pull together." The people who work at this center help teenagers go to college so they can then go on to help others.**

Home Security

When we trust in God's care, His peace helps us not to worry.

Materials
- Bible with a bookmark at Psalm 29:11
- items people use for home security (warning sign, lock, keys, light, etc.)

> **The LORD gives strength to his people; the LORD blesses his people with peace.**
>
> Psalm 29:11

Introduction
When we trust in God's care, the peace He gives us will help us not to worry. Let's find out how some people trusted in God and how God helped them in a very scary situation.

Presentation
1. Show the items you brought. **What do people use these items for? What are some other things people depend on to protect them?** Let the children respond. **Two missionaries, John Paton and his wife, knew one night they needed protection.**

2. **John Paton and his wife were missionaries in the late 1800s on Tanna, an island near the country of Australia. One tribe didn't like the missionaries and wanted to kill them. Late one night the Patons realized angry warriors from this tribe had surrounded their home. All night long the Patons prayed to God. In the morning the warriors were gone! The Patons thanked God for keeping them safe. About a year later, the tribal chief who had planned the attack became a Christian. The chief asked John who the men were the chief had seen guarding the missionary home the night of the attack. John told the chief he and his wife were the only people there. Both men then realized the warriors had seen angels God sent to protect the missionaries.**

Conclusion
Read Psalm 29:11 aloud. **What does this verse say God does? What does it mean to say we have God's peace?** (We can feel safe because we know God always cares for us.) **How did the Patons show they believed this about God?** Children can respond. Lead the children in prayer.

Discussion Questions

1. **What are some scary situations kids your age often face? What do you know about God that might help someone in a situation like this to have peace?**

2. **What are some ways God has cared for you or for someone you know?** Describe one or more ways God has cared for you before asking the children to respond.

3. **How can you remember to trust God's care when you are worried or afraid?** (pray, read a Bible verse, talk to someone who loves God)

Additional Information for Older Children

When John Paton became a missionary, one of the first things he had to do was learn the language of the people on the island of Tanna. Their language, Tannese, had never been written down! But John thought of a way to write down the words. He was even able to print the Bible for the people of Tanna. John later wrote the story of his life in a book titled *John G. Paton, Missionary to the Cannibals*.

Our Daily Bread

We can have peace because God knows what we need and promises to care for us.

Materials

- Bible with a bookmark at John 14:27
- loaf of bread
- carton of milk

> **Peace I leave with you; my peace I give you. I do not give to you as the world gives. Do not let your hearts be troubled and do not be afraid.**
>
> John 14:27

Introduction

God knows just what we need, and He promises to take care of us! Because we can depend on God, we can have peace. Let's find out how one man showed he had peace and trusted God.

Presentation

1. **What is your favorite breakfast food?** Children can respond. Show the bread and milk. **People often eat bread and milk as part of their breakfast. Let's find out about some children who didn't know if they would have any food to eat for breakfast.**

2. **In the early 1800s, George Müller was a preacher in England. George was also the leader of an orphanage for poor children. One morning the tables in the orphanage dining room were set, but there was no food and no money to buy food. George didn't know where he would get food for breakfast. George and the children prayed, "Dear Father, thank You for what You are going to give us to eat." As soon as they finished praying, the town baker knocked at the door. He had loaves of fresh bread! The baker had gotten up early to make bread because he felt God wanted him to give this gift to the children at the orphanage. A moment later, there was another knock at the door. The milkman's cart had broken down outside the orphanage, and he needed to empty the cart before he could repair it. The milk would be wasted, so he offered to give the milk to the children. Time after time, God answered George's prayers just like this! George and the orphans had peace because they trusted God's care.**

Conclusion

Read John 14:27 aloud. **How did God care for George Müller and the orphans?** Accept responses. **What are some other ways God cares for people?** Lead the children in prayer, thanking God for taking care of us so we can have peace and depend on Him.

Discussion Questions

1. **What are some things a kid your age might worry about?** (a test in school, a sick parent or grandparent, being liked by others)

2. **What can kids do if they are feeling worried about something?** (remember God's promise to care for us, tell God what they are worried about, read in God's Word about how He takes care of His family)

3. **What does Jesus tell us about worrying?** (There is no need to worry, because God knows what we need and will provide for us.)

4. **How can we get the peace Jesus said He left with us?** (We can ask Jesus to forgive our sins, tell Him that we want to be members of God's family, and keep trusting God even when we're worried.) Talk to interested children about salvation (see "Leading a Child to Christ" on p. 8).

Additional Information for Older Children

Before George Müller opened his orphanage, only rich children were allowed to stay in England's orphanages. George said he opened his orphanage for two reasons: he wanted to care for poor orphans, and he wanted to show that God would supply the needs of anyone who prayed and trusted in Him. More than 10,000 boys and girls were cared for because George prayed and trusted God.

Peace in the Congo

Because God has forgiven us through Christ, encourage people to forgive each other and make peace.

> **Be like-minded, be sympathetic, love one another, be compassionate and humble.**
>
> 1 Peter 3:8

Materials

- Bible with a bookmark at 1 Peter 3:8
- world map

Introduction

We can encourage people to forgive each other and make peace, because God has forgiven us. Let's find out about one man who worked hard to help people and make peace.

Presentation

1. Show children the map. **Where is the country in which we live?** A volunteer can locate the country on the map. Show the children or ask an older child to find the country of the Democratic Republic of the Congo (formerly Zaire). **William Sheppard was an African American missionary to the Congo in 1890. He went to this country because many of the tribes of people who lived there did not know about Jesus.**

2. William learned the different languages the people in the Congo spoke and helped the people build churches, schools, and homes for children. William even became friends with a tribe of people who had always killed any outsiders who came to their area. William's work with these people made him so famous that he was invited three times to the White House, home of the president of the United States. William could have felt like he had done enough to help the people in the Congo, but he knew there was a lot more important work left to do. At that time, the king of the Kingdom of Belgium was in control of the Congo. His soldiers forced many people in the Congo to work under terrible conditions. William began to write about the problems he saw. Soon people all around the world learned about these problems and convinced the king of Belgium to treat the people in the Congo in better ways.

Conclusion

Read 1 Peter 3:8 aloud. **Which instructions in this verse tell ways to make peace?** Accept responses. **How did William Sheppard obey this verse? How can you make peace with others? Let's ask God to help us encourage people to forgive each other and make peace.** Lead the children in prayer. **Making peace with others is a good way to show that we love God and are members of His family.** Talk with interested children about becoming members of God's family (see "Leading a Child to Christ" on p. 8).

Discussion Questions

1. People can live in harmony with each other ("be like-minded") when they choose to respect each other. What can you do to show more respect and kindness to your friends? Your family?

2. How do you think living in harmony, or respecting each other, can make peace?

3. Forgiving others is one way to live in harmony with others. What can a kid your age do when it seems difficult to forgive others? (ask for God's help, read about God's forgiveness in the Bible, forgive even when it's hard)

Additional Information for Older Children

William Sheppard's wife, Lucy Gantt Sheppard, traveled with her husband to the Congo. She worked hard to help the people in the Congo have a good education. Lucy wrote books in the language of the people who lived in the Congo. She wrote the very first reading book written in their language.

Prison Peace

Working to make peace helps us build friendships.

Materials

- Bible with a bookmark at Colossians 3:15
- bell or other item used as signal for quiet

> **Let the peace of Christ rule in your hearts, since as members of one body you were called to peace.**
>
> Colossians 3:15

Introduction

When we do our best to make peace, it helps us make friends. Let's find out how one woman worked to make peace and what happened as a result.

Presentation

1. Get the children's attention by ringing the bell or using the other item you brought. **If you were trying to signal a crowd of fighting people to be quiet, what would you do? Volunteers can answer. In 1932 a woman named Gladys Aylward was asked to quiet down a crowd of fighting prisoners.**

2. **Gladys Aylward had moved from England to China so she could tell people about Jesus. "People who trust Jesus don't need to be afraid," Gladys said. One day at a nearby prison, a fight among the prisoners was so bad the soldiers were afraid to go into the prison to stop the fight! The** governor of that area remembered what Gladys had said and asked her to make peace among the prisoners. Gladys walked into the prison courtyard and shouted for quiet. When the men quieted down, Gladys asked them to tell her why they were fighting. "This prison is crowded and the prisoners have nothing to do," the men said. "We fight over food because we don't have enough to eat." As Gladys talked and listened to the men, they agreed to make peace and stop fighting. Then Gladys worked hard to help keep peace among the prisoners. She even found a way for the prisoners to earn money so they could buy enough food.

Conclusion

Read Colossians 3:15 aloud. **When we have Christ's peace in our hearts, it means we do our best to avoid or stop fights and arguments. How did Gladys Aylward help stop fights?** (She listened to the men in the prison and helped them settle their arguments.) **Let's ask God to help us make peace with others.** Lead the children in prayer.

Discussion Questions

1. **When are some times kids your age have to work to make peace at school? At home?** (when friends are arguing, when brothers or sisters are angry)

2. **When have you seen someone else work to make peace? What happened?** Tell your own example of a situation in which working to make peace resulted in friendship.

3. **When are some times people might need help to make peace?** (when they are too mad to talk to each other, when they don't understand each other)

4. **How can we get God's help when we're working to make peace?** (pray to God, read His Word, ask for help from older people who love God)

Additional Information for Older Children

Before Gladys Aylward went to China, no one thought she would be a good missionary. But Gladys refused to give up her plan to be a missionary. She worked hard and saved money until she was able to buy a ticket to China. In China, God helped Gladys learn to speak the difficult Chinese language and to become a great missionary.

Praise and Worship

Branches of Praise
God gives us everything we need.

> My God will meet all your needs according to the riches of his glory in Christ Jesus.
>
> Philippians 4:19

Materials
- Bible with a bookmark at Philippians 4:19
- several tree branches
- objects used at sporting events—pom-pom, pennant, foam hand, etc.—specific branches names, lemon *(optional)*

Introduction
It's important to remember all God has done for us. In the Old Testament God's people celebrated the Feast (or Festival) of Tabernacles (or Booths) to help them remember how God took care of them when they left Egypt. Let's find out some of the things they used in this celebration and learn how the celebration got its name.

Presentation
1. Show the branches. **At the Feast of Tabernacles, called Sukkot (suh-KOHT) in Hebrew, God told His people to gather different types of tree branches and fruit.** *(Optional: Read Leviticus 23:40 aloud.)* **The branches and fruit were used in several ways. One way was to decorate small booths (that is, shelters) the people built. Traditionally, the people lived in these booths for the seven days of the celebration. Living in the booths reminded them of the time after they escaped from Egypt, when they had no houses to live in. The word *Sukkot* means "tabernacles" or "booths," and that's why this celebration was called the Feast of Tabernacles.** *(Optional: Read Leviticus 23:42 aloud.)* **Even today Jewish people build and decorate booths as part of this holiday.**

2. **Besides being used to decorate the booths, the branches were used to show praise to God. What are some objects people use to cheer for or praise a sports team?** Accept responses. *(Optional: Display objects used at sporting events.)* Invite volunteers to wave branches (or hands) in the following traditional pattern for Sukkot: to the front, sides, back, up, and down. **The branches were waved in all directions to show that God is ruler over all the earth.**

Conclusion

We can praise God too—and not just on certain holidays, but all year long. Read Philippians 4:19 aloud. **What does this verse tell us about God?** Volunteers can answer. **This verse tells us a good reason to celebrate!** Pray, thanking God for giving us all that we need.

Discussion Questions

1. **What are some times in the Bible when God gave people what they needed?** (manna and water to the Israelites in the desert, a dry sea for the Israelites to get away from Pharaoh, instructions for Noah to build an ark so he could be safe during the flood)

2. **With the things God has given us, how can He use us to help provide for other people's needs?** (share what you have with people who need it, help serve food to people at a homeless shelter, give an offering at church so the church can use the money to help people with their needs)

3. **In what ways can you thank God for giving you everything you need?** (pray, tell others about His gifts, sing songs of praise to God)

Additional Information for Older Children

Traditionally, branches from three trees—myrtle, willow, and palm—were collected at the Feast of Tabernacles. *(Optional: Show one or more of the named branches.)* **The branches were braided together and then waved in the air as a way of praising God. A fruit—called a citron—was also held and waved. A citron looks like a lemon.** *(Optional: Show a lemon.)* **In Hebrew, the branches were called a lulav** (LOO-lahv) **and the fruit was called the etrog** (EH-trog).

Cheerful Praise

Use your abilities to give praise to God.

Materials

- Bible with a bookmark at Psalm 136
- objects used to cheer sports teams (pom-poms, pennants, large foam fingers, etc.)

> **Give thanks to the LORD, for he is good. His love endures forever.**
>
> Psalm 136:1

Introduction

We can give praise to God when we use the abilities and talents He gave us. Let's look at a way people praised God in Old Testament times.

Presentation

1. **When a sports team scores a goal, what does the crowd do?** (cheers) Display the objects used to cheer sports teams.

2. **Because God is so good to us and because He loves us so much, we want to cheer for joy! One meaning of the word** *cheer* **is "to praise someone or something." The book of Psalms is a book of praise songs. The writers of the psalms used their abilities and talents to praise God.**

3. **Psalm 136 is a psalm written in an interesting way. After each sentence said by the Old Testament song leader, the choir or worshippers would say, "His love endures forever." What does it mean when the psalm says "His love endures forever"?** (It will never end. God will always love us.) Lead a reading of Psalm 136 in the manner described (read or ask an older child to read the verses, and lead the children in saying the refrain "His love endures forever").

Conclusion

Because God loves us so much, He gives us abilities that we can use to celebrate and praise Him. Pray, thanking God for the abilities He gives us.

Discussion Questions

1. **How have you seen people at church use their abilities to praise God?** (make banners, sing songs, play music)

2. **What are some things kids your age can do to praise God? What abilities do you have that you could use to praise and worship God?**

3. **Why do you think praising God is important?**

Additional Information for Older Children

When things are scary or difficult, it may seem hard to praise God. But in the Old Testament, we can read about King Jehoshaphat and how he praised God even when three different armies were coming against his country! To show they believed God's promise to fight the battle for them, the king and his people chose singers instead of soldiers to lead the army! The singers didn't carry swords—mabye they carried cymbals and harps and other instruments! Read what happened in 2 Chronicles 20:20–22, 27–28.

Foreign Phrases

Because Jesus is God's Son, we can worship Him as King now and forever.

> **The LORD will be king over the whole earth. On that day there will be one LORD, and his name the only name.**
>
> Zechariah 14:9

Materials
- Bible with a bookmark at Zechariah 14:9
- large sheet of paper or whiteboard
- marker
- world map or globe

Preparation

On a large sheet of paper or whiteboard, print the following language names and phrases—English: Jesus is Lord; Spanish: Jesús es Señor (HAY-soos ehs seh-NYOHR); French: Jesus est le Seigneur (JHAY-soo eh leh seh-NYOOR); Tagalog (Philippines): Si Hesus ay Panginoon (SEH hay-SOOS ay PAH-nee-nah-ahn); German: Herr (YAY-soos eest HEHR); Italian: Il Jesus é il Signore (EEL HAY-soos eh eel seeg-NOH-ree). Practice saying the phrases.

Introduction

People all over the world can praise and worship Jesus. They worship Jesus as Lord of their lives. They worship Jesus as King of heaven and earth for all time. Let's find out what some Christians around the world might say to worship Jesus.

Presentation

1. **The Bible tells us one day, everybody on the earth will say Jesus is Lord.** *Lord* is a special name for Jesus that shows He is Ruler or King of all things and of all people. *(Optional: Read Philippians 2:9–11 aloud.)* **At our church, we speak English when we say "Jesus is Lord."** Show the map or globe and point out the area where your church is located.

2. **People in each country of the world say these words in their own languages.** Show what you prepared with "Jesus is Lord" written in several languages. Point to the Spanish words. **This is how people say "Jesus is Lord" in Spanish.** Repeat for each language, including any languages spoken by the children in your group. On the map or globe, find locations where each language is spoken as you help children pronounce the phrases.

Conclusion

Read Zechariah 14:9. **This verse talks about the day when Jesus returns to earth. Then everyone will understand Jesus really is the King. How would you explain to a friend what this verse means?** Volunteers can share ideas. Close in prayer, inviting children to call out "Jesus is Lord" in any of the languages you have written.

Discussion Questions

1. **What does it mean to say that Jesus is our King?** (We want to love and obey Him. He is our Ruler.)

2. **When can we worship Jesus as King?** (when we pray, when we sing songs of praise, when we talk about Jesus to others)

3. **Why is it important to worship Jesus?** (to show our love to Him, to help others worship Him too)

4. **What can we do to show we believe Jesus is King and worship Him?** (We can obey what the Bible tells us to do; sing songs of praise to Him; and give Him offerings of love, time, and money.)

Additional Information for Older Children

Kings or leaders of countries sometimes gain power because they lead their armies into war. Jesus' war was not against people or countries but against sin and death and against God's enemy, Satan. By dying on the cross and rising from the dead, Jesus won the war against all the sin in the world. The Bible tells us that one day all people will recognize that Jesus is the King of Kings.

Magnificent Music

We can worship God for His love and His promise to send the Savior.

Materials

- Bible with a bookmark at Luke 1:46–55
- rhythm instruments
- recording of "The Magnificat," music player *(optional)*

> **My soul glorifies the Lord and my spirit rejoices in God my Savior.**
>
> Luke 1:46–47

Introduction

God's love and His promise to send a Savior are good reasons to worship Him! Singing is one important way people worship God. Let's find out about one of the oldest songs ever sung about Jesus' birth.

Presentation

1. **What are some songs that people sing at Christmas?** ("Silent Night," "Jingle Bells," "Away in a Manger," etc.) Use rhythm instruments to play the rhythms to several Christmas songs. Ask children to guess the names of the songs. *(Optional: Lead the children in singing one or more of the songs.)*

2. **All these songs are sung at Christmastime, but the very first Christmas song was sung by Mary after the angel told her she was going to be Jesus' mother. The words of Mary's song are now part of a song called "The Magnificat"** (mahg-NEE-fee-kaht), **which is a Latin word. "The Magnificat" is sung in many churches, not just at Christmastime, but all year long. The words of Mary's song are said to have been set to music more often than any other hymn!** Read or ask several children to take turns reading Luke 1:46–47. *(Optional: Also read verses 48–50 and/or play a portion of "The Magnificat.")*

3. **What did Mary praise God for in this song?** (for being her Savior, for doing great things for her, for His mercy) **How is this song the same or different from the other Christmas songs we named?** Volunteers can respond.

Conclusion

The word *magnificat* means "to magnify." When we magnify God, we are praising Him and telling others how wonderful He is. Pray, praising God for His wonderful gift of His Son, Jesus. Talk with interested children about becoming members of God's family (see "Leading a Child to Christ" on p. 8).

Discussion Questions

1. **What are some reasons to worship and thank God at Christmastime?** (He showed His love by sending Jesus as our Savior. He promised a Savior for many years.)

2. **What are some ways to worship God at Christmastime?** (We can thank God in prayer and song for sending Jesus, show God's love to others by giving gifts, and put up decorations that are reminders of Jesus' birth.)

3. **What is one way you would like to worship God this week?**

4. **How do giving gifts and receiving gifts help us celebrate Jesus' birth?** (Jesus is God's gift to us.)

Additional Information for Older Children

Mary's song of praise is similar to a song sung by Hannah in the Old Testament. Mary sang her song to praise God for the great things He had done for His people and for loving her and allowing her to be the mother of Jesus, the Savior of the world. In a similar way, Hannah was praising God for giving her a son, Samuel, who would be dedicated to God's work. Invite children to read some or all of Hannah's song in 1 Samuel 2:1–10.

Praise Parade

God's family celebrates and praises God together!

Materials
- Bible with bookmarks at Psalm 24 and 149:1
- large sheet of paper or whiteboard
- marker
- objects used at parades—like confetti, balloons, batons, whistles, drums, etc. *(optional)*

> **Praise the LORD. Sing to the LORD a new song, his praise in the assembly of his faithful people.**
>
> Psalm 149:1

Preparation
On the large sheet of paper or whiteboard, draw one line for each letter of the name of several objects used at parades (see suggested list above). *(Optional: Use objects associated with specific parades in your community.)*

Introduction
When God's family gets together, we celebrate and praise God! Let's look at one way big crowds of people get together and celebrate special occasions.

Presentation
1. Display what you have written. Invite volunteers to suggest letters of the alphabet. As volunteers suggest letters, print the letters on the correct lines. If a letter is not used in any of the words you are using, write the letter at the bottom of the paper or whiteboard. As letters fill in the words, let children guess what the words are. **All these words are the names of things used at a special event. Guess what the event is!** Volunteers can respond until the event, a parade, is revealed.

2. **Another word like *parade* is *procession*. A procession is a group of people moving forward together, usually as part of a very special ceremony. Processions are an important part of funerals, graduations, and weddings. Often, music accompanies processions. Psalm 24 is a song that was written for the procession David led when he brought the ark of the covenant to Jerusalem. (The ark was a special box that reminded the people of God's presence.)** Read or ask an older child to read Psalm 24:7–10 aloud. *(Optional: As the verses are read, have the children walk in a procession around the room.)*

Conclusion

When David brought the ark to Jerusalem, the Israelites celebrated and praised God. As members of God's family, we can celebrate and praise God too! Read Psalm 149:1 aloud. **An assembly is a large group of people. When are some times large groups of people come together to praise God?** Pray, thanking God the members of His family can celebrate and praise Him together.

Discussion Questions

1. **What has God given you to show His love for you? How has God given you courage? When has God forgiven you?** Accept responses.

2. **Why is it important to celebrate these gifts God gives us?** (to recognize God's constant goodness to His people, to remember the good gifts God gives us every day)

3. **What are some ways to praise God with other members of His family?**

4. **What is one way you can praise God with your family this week?** (sing a praise song together before eating dinner, each person in the family thanks God for something when you pray together, make a poster that tells God reasons you love Him)

Additional Information for Older Children

Many psalms were written for special occasions. **Psalm 132 may have been written for two occasions: the temple dedication** (children can compare Psalm 132:8–10 to 2 Chronicles 6:41–42) **and when the king was crowned** (children can read Psalm 132:18).

Sing a Song

Worship God with joy because of the great things He has done.

Materials

- Bible with a bookmark at Psalm 100:2
- recording of "Hark! The Herald Angels Sing" and music player or copies of words and music
- large sheet of paper or whiteboard
- marker
- hymnal

> **Worship the LORD with gladness; come before him with joyful songs.**
>
> Psalm 100:2

Introduction

God has done so many great things! We can joyfully worship God when we think about the great things God has done. Let's find out about one man who worshipped God and helped others worship God too.

Presentation

1. Invite the children to sing or listen to "Hark! The Herald Angels Sing." **When do we usually sing this song? What does this song say about Jesus?** Children can respond. **A man named Charles Wesley wrote this song and many other songs about Jesus.**

2. **Charles Wesley grew up in a very big family in England in the 1700s. He went to church and did many good things all his life, but he didn't really understand what it meant to be a Christian or how much God loved him. When Charles was a grown-up, he lived with some Christians in London. While he was there, Charles saw how kind and gentle they were, and he heard them talk about how they lived as part of God's family. Those Christians helped Charles understand God's love for him. Charles was so glad to know of God's love that he began to write songs about God's love and forgiveness. For many years Charles and his brother, John, preached and sang about God's love and forgiveness to people all over England. Charles eventually wrote 6,000 hymns! Many people learned to love and worship God because of Charles's music and preaching.**

Conclusion

Read Psalm 100:2 aloud. **How did Charles Wesley show his joy for the great things God has done?** (He wrote and sang songs about God.) **What are some things God has done for which you are thankful?** List the children's responses on a large sheet of paper or whiteboard. Lead the children in prayer, thanking God for items children listed.

Discussion Questions

1. **How do people often show they are joyful or happy?** (smile, sing)

2. **How can we show joy when we worship God?** (We can sing songs that tell of God's greatness, tell others about the ways in which God helps us, and thank God in prayer for the good things He gives us.)

3. **What is one way we have worshipped God today?**

Additional Information for Older Children

"Hark! The Herald Angels Sing" is often sung to celebrate Jesus' birth. Another of the hymns Charles Wesley wrote is often sung to celebrate Jesus' resurrection. Ask volunteers to take turns reading one or more stanzas of "Christ the Lord Is Risen Today" from a hymnal. **What words from this song help us tell about our joy that Jesus is alive?**

Thumb Wrap!

Believing in God and His power makes us want to worship Him.

Materials

- Bible with a bookmark at Psalm 95:6–7
- masking tape
- a variety of objects (pencil, paper, book, cup of water, marker, paper clip)

> **Come, let us bow down in worship, let us kneel before the Lord our Maker; for he is our God.**
>
> Psalm 95:6–7

Introduction

Getting to know what God is like helps us believe in Him and worship Him. Try this experiment with me to learn about a special way God made us that shows His great power.

Presentation

1. With masking tape, wrap together the thumb and first finger of a volunteer's writing hand. Then ask the volunteer to try to write his or her name on a piece of paper.

2. Repeat with other volunteers and these tasks: turn the pages of a book, drink a cup of water, pick up a paper clip, open a door, button or unbutton a coat or sweater, etc.

3. Discuss the activity by asking, **What made your task so hard to do? What would happen if you didn't have a thumb? What would happen if you only had thumbs on your hands?** Accept responses.

Conclusion

God made our fingers and thumbs to work just right. Listen to these verses that talk about God as the one who made us. Read Psalm 95:6–7 aloud. **One way to worship God is by thanking Him for making us.** Lead children in prayer, thanking God for making us in such special ways.

Discussion Questions

1. **What are some other special ways that God has made us?** (We can taste different flavors. Our arms and legs have joints so they can bend.)

2. **What's something about the way you're made for which you want to thank God?** Tell children something you're glad God has made you able to do.

3. **What are some of the ways people in our church thank and worship God?** (sing songs of praise, pray, tell others about God's greatness)

Wave Bottles

Knowing Jesus more makes us want to praise Him.

Materials
- Bible with a bookmark at Psalm 145:3
- 12-oz clear plastic bottle
- water
- blue food coloring
- mineral oil
- tape
- materials to make additional bottles, picture of ocean or starry sky *(optional)*

> **Great is the LORD and most worthy of praise; his greatness no one can fathom.**
>
> Psalm 145:3

Preparation
Fill the bottle half full with water. Add several drops of blue food coloring. Fill the remainder of the bottle with mineral oil. Fasten the cap tightly and wrap with tape. (If you have a large group, prepare more than one bottle.)

Introduction
The more we get to know about Jesus, the more we want to praise Him. Let's look at something that reminds us of how great Jesus is.

Presentation
1. Show the bottle. Ask a volunteer to hold the bottle horizontally and gently tilt the bottle from end to end, creating a wavelike motion. Allow time for children to experiment with the bottle.

2. **The waves in this bottle remind me of the ocean. What words would you use to describe an ocean? How hard do you think it might be to see to the very bottom of the ocean or a deep lake? Why?** Accept responses. *(Optional: Show a picture of the ocean instead of using the wave bottle, or show a starry sky picture and talk with children about the impossibility of counting all the stars in the sky.)*

Conclusion
The ocean is so big and so deep we can't understand exactly what it is like. Listen to what the Bible says about the Lord. Read Psalm 145:3 aloud. **The word *fathom* means "understand." This verse tells us the Lord is so great we can never understand exactly how great He is! Because Jesus is so great, we want to praise Him.** Lead the children in prayer, thanking Jesus for His greatness.

Discussion Questions

1. **What are some other things that remind us of how great Jesus is?** (the miracles He did on earth, His resurrection)

2. **What are some of the ways people praise Jesus for His greatness?** (sing songs about Him, pray, tell others about His greatness)

3. **What would you like to praise Jesus for?**

Welcoming Ways
Jesus is so great we can't help but praise Him.

Materials
- Bible with a bookmark at Psalm 147:1
- objects used to welcome and praise others—medal, red carpet, confetti, pennants, pom-poms, etc. *(optional)*

> **Praise the LORD. How good it is to sing praises to our God, how pleasant and fitting to praise him!**
> Psalm 147:1

Introduction
We can't help but praise and honor Jesus because He is so great! Let's look at some of the ways great people are honored.

Presentation
1. One at a time, pantomime, or ask volunteers to pantomime, ways to praise or honor people. (Lay out a red carpet, drop flower petals down an aisle, cheer for a sports team, salute, bow, curtsy, throw confetti, etc.) As each action is pantomimed, let children guess the action. **Who might be honored that way?** *(Optional: Show objects used to honor others, and ask the children to describe how these objects could be used to praise others.)*

2. **Why do we do special things to praise people?** (to show they are important to us, to show that we admire or love them) **On the first Palm Sunday, people praised and honored Jesus when He arrived in Jerusalem. They clapped and cheered, waved palm branches in the air, and laid palm branches and their coats on the road for Jesus to ride on. Every year we remember and celebrate Palm Sunday because it was the beginning of the time when Jesus died for our sins and then rose again to give us new life.**

Conclusion
During the week that followed Jesus' kingly parade into Jerusalem, Jesus died on the cross to make a way for all of us to become members of God's family. He deserves all the honor we can give Him! Read Psalm 147:1 aloud. **What are some of the things God has done in your life for which you would like to praise and honor Him?** Praise God in prayer, mentioning the children's responses.

Discussion Questions

1. **What are some of the reasons we want to praise Jesus?** (He is God's Son. He was willing to die on the cross to pay the punishment for all people's sins. He rose from the dead. He loves us all. He taught us the best way to live.)

2. **What are some ways we can praise Jesus?** (We can sing songs to Him. When we pray, we can tell Him why we love Him or what we are thankful for. We can tell others how wonderful He is.)

3. **What is your favorite way to praise Jesus?** Volunteers can respond.

Additional Information for Older Children

We may not think of a donkey as a royal animal; but in Bible times, the donkey was considered a sign of humility, peace, and royalty! Read 1 Kings 1:38–40 to learn about a kingly parade similar to the one we celebrate on Palm Sunday. In Zechariah 9:9, you can read the Old Testament prophet Zechariah's prediction of a King coming to save God's people—riding on a donkey! Now we know the King he wrote about was Jesus! Ask a volunteer to read the verse aloud.

Prayer

Ask God!
Pray to God every day.

Pray continually, give thanks in all circumstances.

1 Thessalonians 5:17–18

Materials

- Bible with a bookmark at 1 Thessalonians 5:17–18
- flashlight with batteries
- plant
- votive candle
- match
- wide-mouthed jar
- snack for each child

Introduction

If we want to get to know God and obey Him, we need to talk to Him every day. Let's look at these objects and talk about what they need in order to work.

Presentation

1. Show the flashlight and ask children to tell what it needs to work. (batteries) **What are some other items that need batteries in order to work?** (handheld video games, toys, etc.)

2. Show the plant and ask children to tell what it needs to grow. (water, sunlight) **What are some other things that need water and sunlight to grow?** (trees, flowers, etc.)

3. Light the candle. **What does this candle need in order to burn?** (oxygen) Cover the candle with the jar and watch to see the candle flame go out. Repeat the experiment, inviting children to count how long it takes for the flame to go out.

4. **What do you need to do every day in order to live and grow?** (eat food, drink water, breathe air) Serve a snack to each child.

Conclusion

We've talked about what all these items need. What does 1 Thessalonians 5:17–18 say we need to do? Read the verses aloud. **Sometimes we only think about praying to God when we have a problem or need something. But when does 1 Thessalonians 5:17–18 say we should pray? Talking to God every day about what we are doing and the choices we are making helps us love and obey Him.** Lead children in prayer, thanking God that we can talk to Him.

Discussion Questions

1. When can you talk to God?

2. What are some things a kid your age could tell God about school?

3. Who might help you remember to pray?

4. What's something you'd like to thank God for right now?

Light Lesson
Prayer helps us get to know Jesus, God's Son.

Materials
- Bible with bookmarks at Matthew 17:2 and Psalm 69:13
- sheet of white paper
- marker
- flashlight

> Let us not love with words or speech but with actions and in truth.
>
> 1 John 3:18

Preparation
Fold the paper in half. Draw a sun on the folded paper.

Introduction
We can get to know Jesus, God's Son, when we pray. One time when three of Jesus' disciples were praying with Him, they learned Jesus was God's Son. Let's find out what happened.

Presentation

1. Holding paper so the drawing faces you, shine the flashlight directly on the blank side of the paper. **When I shine this light directly on the sheet of paper, what do you see?** (nothing but the paper) **Without moving the paper, move the light source behind the paper. When I shine the light from behind the paper, what do you see?** (the sun drawn on the paper)

2. **The Bible tells us about a time when light made Jesus' disciples see Him in a different way. His face shone as bright as the sun and made them know He was God's Son. Jesus' appearance changed so much that the Bible says He was transfigured. The word** *transfigure* **means "to change."** Read or ask an older child to read Matthew 17:2. **Many. churches remember Jesus' transfiguration on a special Sunday each year. Celebrating this event reminds God's followers that Jesus is God's Son, the Savior sent by God.**

Conclusion
We can get to know Jesus by reading about Him in the Bible. We also get to know Jesus through prayer. In the same way you become better friends with others by talking with them, you get to know Jesus better whenever you pray. Read Psalm 69:13 aloud. **The writer of this verse is praying to God because he knows God loves him and will answer his prayers.** Pray, thanking God for Jesus, His Son, and asking God's help in getting to know who Jesus is. Talk with children about becoming Christians (see "Leading a Child to Christ" on p. 8).

Discussion Questions

1. **What are some things you know about Jesus?** (He is God's Son. He loves us. He is always with us.) **How have you gotten to know who Jesus is?** (from teachers and parents, from reading God's Word)

2. **Why do you think praying helps us get to know Jesus?** (When we pray, it reminds us of Jesus' love and care for us.)

3. **What kinds of things can you talk to Jesus about?**

4. **When are some times you pray every day? When are some other times you can pray?**

Additional Information for Older Children

About a week prior to Jesus' transfiguration on the mountain, Jesus asked His disciples who people thought He was. Jesus also asked who *they* thought He was. Read what Peter said in Matthew 16:13–16.

The Bells Are Ringing

When we talk to God, we can worship Him for who He is and what He has done.

Materials
- Bible with bookmarks at Psalm 100 and Daniel 2:20
- bells
- pictures of bells *(optional)*

Introduction
For all God is and all He has done, we can worship God by talking to Him. Let's look at a way to know it is time to come together and worship God.

Presentation

1. Display the bells you brought. *(Optional: Show pictures of bells.)* Allow volunteers to ring the bells. **Bells often tell people when it's time to do something. What kinds of bells can you think of that tell you it's time for something?** (school bells, dinner bells, customer service bells, Emergency Broadcast System warning bells, church bells) **Many churches have bell towers and bells that are rung to let people know it is time for a worship service.**

2. **When God's followers come together, they sometimes read verses from the Bible that tell everyone it's time to worship God. The verses that are read are called a call to worship. Psalm 100 is a call to worship. The words of this psalm help people think about how and why we should worship God.** Ask older volunteers to read the psalm, one verse at a time. At the beginning and end of the psalm, as well as at the end of each verse, invite volunteers to ring the bells as another reminder to worship God.

Conclusion
When Daniel lived, in Bible times, he worshipped God too. Read Daniel 2:20 aloud. What two words does this verse use to describe God? (wisdom and power) **What are some of the ways God's wisdom and power help people today?** (He answers our prayers, gives us courage, and helps us do right.) Pray, thanking God and praising Him for His wisdom and power.

Discussion Questions

1. **Who are some people who often receive praise in our world today?** (athletes, movie stars) **Why is it important to worship and praise God?** (Because God is greater than anyone else, He deserves our worship and praise. We want to tell God we love Him and how glad we are about all the things He has done for us.)

2. **In Psalm 100, the words *gates* and *courts* are referring to places in the temple area where people worshipped God in Bible times. Where are some places we could enter, giving thanks and praise to God?** (church, home, school)

3. **What does Psalm 100 mean by describing God as faithful to "all generations" (a generation is a group of people born at the same time)?** (God has cared for people and loved people all through the history of the world.)

4. **What do you want to praise God for today?** Tell your own answer to this question before inviting volunteers to answer.

Additional Information for Older Children

Many psalms have the words "of David" written at the beginning of the psalm. This phrase could mean David wrote the psalm or the psalm was written by someone else and dedicated to David. Look at these psalms to find who Bible scholars think either wrote the psalm or used the psalm in worship. Children can look at these psalms to find the probable authors: Psalm 19 (David, king of Israel), Psalm 42 (the sons of Korah, a group of musicians), Psalm 50 (Asaph, a choir leader in David's time), Psalm 90 (Moses, leader of God's people when they escaped from Egypt).

Watch and Wait

God always answers prayer—sometimes in ways we don't expect.

Materials
- Bible with a bookmark at Colossians 4:2
- newspapers
- paper plate
- glue
- salt in a shaker
- paintbrush
- watercolor paint
- container of water
- extra materials for children to try the experiment *(optional)*

> **Devote yourselves to prayer, being watchful and thankful.**
>
> Colossians 4:2

Preparation
Make a practice design, following the directions below.

Introduction
Sometimes when something takes a long time to happen, we get tired of waiting and watching for it to happen. When we pray to God, we need to wait and watch to see Him answer our prayers. Watch to see what happens in this experiment.

Presentation
1. Cover a table or an area of the floor with newspapers. Squeeze glue onto a paper plate, creating a design of thick lines that intersect.

2. Immediately pour salt onto the lines, making sure to cover the glue completely. Shake any excess salt onto the glue. Saturate the paintbrush with water so that it is very wet. Then dab watercolor paint onto one of the lines, holding the brush at one place. The color will move along the lines as the salt absorbs the water in the paint. Encourage the children to keep watching to see what happens to the paint.

3. After the color has stopped spreading, rinse the brush in water and apply another color of paint at a different place. The two paints will mix at the point where they meet. **What did you expect would happen? What did happen?**

Small Group Option
Provide materials for children to create their own designs.

Conclusion
Just as we watched to see what would happen with the paint, it's up to us to keep watching to find out how God will answer our prayers. We know God will always keep His promise to answer our prayers. Read Colossians 4:2 aloud. **When we devote ourselves to prayer, we never give up praying and looking to see how God will answer our prayers. Sometimes God answers our prayers in ways we don't expect.** Lead children in prayer, thanking God for always hearing and answering our prayers.

Discussion Questions
1. **What are some things kids your age often talk to God about?** (when help is needed to do something, to thank Him for having something good or for something good happening)

2. **Why might God answer a prayer by saying "no" or "later"?** (God knows what's best for us.)

3. **In what way has God answered a prayer for you or someone in your family?**

4. **What's something you want to talk to God about?**

Worldwide Prayer

We can learn the best way to pray from Jesus' examples.

Materials

- Bible with bookmarks at Matthew 6:9 and Philippians 4:6
- large sheet of paper or whiteboard
- marker
- globe or world map, pictures of flags from countries listed below *(optional)*

> **Do not be anxious about anything, but in every situation, by prayer and petition, with thanksgiving, present your requests to God.**
>
> Philippians 4:6

Preparation

On a large sheet of paper or whiteboard, print one or more of the following: Spanish—Nuestro Padre en el cielo (nyoo-EH-stroh PAH-dreh een ehl see-EH-loh); French—Notre Père dans le ciel (NOH-treh PEHR dahn leh SEE-ehl); German—Unser Vater in Himmel (OON-suhr VAH-tuhr ihn HIHM-uhl); Tagalog (Philippines)—Ama Namin sumasa-langit ka (Ah-mah NAH-meen soo-MAH-sah LAHN-geet kah); Norwegian—Våre Far inne himmelen (VAHR FAHR IHN-eh HIH-meh-lehn); Afrikaans (South Africa)—Ons Vader in hemel (AHNS VAH-duhr ihn HIHM-uhl); Kwazulu (South Africa)—Ubaba Wethu Ebhakabhaka (OO-bah-bah WEE-thoo EHB-hah-kahb-hah-kah). Practice saying the phrases which mean "Our Father in heaven."

Introduction

When Jesus lived on earth, He taught us how to talk to God. One prayer Jesus prayed, called the Lord's Prayer, is prayed by people all over the world. Let's find out about some of the first words in this prayer and practice saying them in different languages.

Norway

Presentation

1. **When Jesus taught the disciples to pray, what name did He use for God?** Read Matthew 6:9 aloud. **Jesus was speaking in the Aramaic language and the word He used for Father was *Abba* (AH-bah). Abba actually means "Daddy"! Jesus showed how much He was loved by His Father in heaven by calling Him Daddy.**

South Africa

2. **Jesus' example shows us we can talk to God as our Daddy too. People in each country of the world say the words of the Lord's Prayer in their own languages.** Show the phrases you prepared. Point to the Spanish words. **This is how people say "Our Father in heaven" in Spanish.** Repeat for each language. Include volunteers in your group who speak other languages. *(Optional: Show a map or globe and identify the locations of the countries named or show pictures of their flags.)*

Conclusion

Read Philippians 4:6. **The word** *anxious* **means "worried." What should we do instead of worry?** (talk to God) Ask children to thank God for His gift of prayer, inviting them to begin with "Our Father in heaven" in any of the languages you practiced.

Discussion Questions

1. **What are some things Jesus prayed about? What did Jesus ask His Father in heaven to do?**

2. **What are some things kids your age worry about?**

3. **How do you think talking to God about your worries will help?** (God will listen to you. He will give you courage. God will remind you that He is with you. God always answers prayer in the very best way.)

4. **What are some things you can thank and praise God for? What are some things you need God to help you with?**

Additional Information for Older Children

When Jesus prayed at Gethsemane on the night He was betrayed by Judas, He again began His prayer with the Aramaic word Abba. Read this prayer in Mark 14:35–36.

Salvation

Bigger Than All
God's love and power are bigger than the biggest fear.

Materials
- Bible with a bookmark at Isaiah 12:2
- 6–8 classroom or household objects ranging in size from very small to very large

Introduction
When we feel worried or afraid because of problems at school or in our neighbor hoods, it helps to remember God's love and power are bigger than our biggest fears. Let's name some things that are bigger than others.

Presentation
1. Invite volunteers to arrange the objects in order of size. Hand volunteers one object each and have them line up in order.

2. Beginning with the smallest object, invite children to name a variety of objects that are bigger than the smallest object but smaller than the next object. For example, a pencil is bigger than a penny but smaller than a book. Continue until all objects have been discussed. **What are the biggest objects you can think of?** (redwood tree, skyscraper, bridge)

Conclusion
We've been talking about a lot of things that are bigger than others. **Listen to Isaiah 12:2 to find out what we can remember about God when we're afraid or worried.** Read Isaiah 12:2 aloud. **We can remember that God's strength and His help for us are bigger than our fears or worries.** Thank God for His love and help when we're worried or afraid.

Discussion Questions

1. What's a worry that a kid your age might have? What's a fear?

2. Why might someone who's afraid forget about God's love and help?

3. How has God helped you when you've felt afraid?

4. What worry or fear do you want to talk to God about?

Breaking Bread Together

Jesus' love for us is so great, He was willing to die on the cross.

Materials
- Bible with bookmarks at John 13:34–35 and 1 John 3:16
- objects used by your church for Communion (plates, cups, chalice, bread or wafers, juice, etc.)
- guest speaker *(optional)*

> **This is how we know what love is: Jesus Christ laid down his life for us.**
> 1 John 3:16

Introduction
Because He loves us so much, Jesus was willing to die on the cross so our sins could be forgiven. The night before He was killed, Jesus ate a special supper with His disciples. Let's look at the way our church family remembers that special supper and Jesus' death on the cross.

Presentation

1. Show the objects one at a time. **What is this object? What are some ways to use it?** *(Optional: Let the children taste the food items.)*

2. **We use these objects when we celebrate the Lord's Supper. One of the names for this celebration is Communion, which means "to share something with others." When we celebrate Communion together, we share in celebrating and remembering the last supper Jesus ate with His disciples before He died on the cross to take the punishment for our sins.** Explain and demonstrate the use of the objects. *(Optional: Invite your pastor or other church leader to talk with children about how your church celebrates the Lord's Supper.)*

3. **One special day each year, many Christians celebrate Jesus' Last Supper with His disciples; this day is called Maundy Thursday. The word *Maundy* comes from a Latin word that means "command."** Read or ask an older child to read John 13:34–35 aloud. **What is the new commandment Jesus gave His followers during the Last Supper?**

Conclusion
Read 1 John 3:16 aloud. **What does this verse tell us that love really is?** (Jesus cares so much for us that He died for us.) Pray, thanking Jesus for dying on the cross for our sins. Talk with interested children about becoming members of God's family (see "Leading a Child to Christ" on p. 8).

Discussion Questions

1. **What are some ways Jesus loved and served people when He was here on earth?** (He healed them, fed them, taught them the best way to live, and washed the disciples' feet.)

2. **How does Jesus show love for us today?** (He answers our prayers and promises to always be with us.)

3. **What are some ways we can show Jesus' love to people today?** (We can be patient with brothers or sisters, help others at school, and play games fairly.)

Additional Information for Older Children

The day on which Jesus died is sometimes called Good Friday. No one knows for sure where the name Good Friday came from. Some people think it came from the phrase "God's Friday." Other people, however, believe the name came about because even though Jesus' death was very sad, so much good happened as a result of His death. What are some of the good things that happened as a result of Jesus' death and resurrection? (Our sins can be forgiven. We can experience God's love.)

Great Greetings

Jesus' death and resurrection make it possible for us to have eternal life.

Materials

- Bible with a bookmark at 1 John 5:11
- music from your collection
- music player

> **God has given us eternal life, and this life is in his Son.**
>
> 1 John 5:11

Introduction

Because Jesus died for our sins and rose again, we can have eternal life! Let's look at one way we remember Jesus' great gift every year at Easter.

Presentation

1. Wave a hand at the children. **What does it mean when I wave my hand at you?** (Waving is a way to say hello or greet someone.) Demonstrate or ask children to demonstrate other ways to greet people. (say hello, give a high five, shake hands)

2. **During Easter, many Christians greet each other in a special way. One person says "Christ is risen," and the other says "He is risen indeed."** For several minutes, play a song as children walk around the room and greet each other in the manner described above. (Note: If there are other Easter traditions followed in your church family, explain these traditions.)

Conclusion

Jesus' resurrection makes it possible for us to become members of God's family! Read 1 John 5:11 aloud. Eternal life means we can live with God in heaven, experiencing His love forever. According to this verse, **where can we get eternal life?** (from God's Son, Jesus) Pray, thanking Jesus for dying on the cross and rising from the dead so we can have eternal life. Talk with interested children about becoming members of God's family (see "Leading a Child to Christ" on p. 8).

Discussion Questions

1. **Why was Jesus the only one who could take the punishment for our sins?** (Jesus is the only person who never sinned. He is the one God promised to send.)

2. **When we choose to become members of God's family, what does He give us?** (forgiveness for our sins, eternal life)

3. **What are some ways we remember Jesus' death and celebrate His resurrection?** (thank Jesus for His love, sing special songs, celebrate Easter with our church families at special worship services)

4. **How does your family celebrate Jesus' resurrection in the Easter season?**

Additional Information for Older Children

Passion Week, also called Holy Week, begins with Palm Sunday and ends with Easter. Many churches are open for services daily or at least on Thursday and Friday as well as Sunday. This is the week during which Lent, which began 40 days earlier, ends. During Lent, many people choose to give up something they like or enjoy, in order to focus more on what Jesus gave up for them.

Joy in Salvation
God's gift of salvation brings great joy.

Materials
- Bible with a bookmark at Habakkuk 3:18
- shoebox with shoes inside

Introduction
When we accept God's gift of salvation, it brings us great joy. Let's find out how one person learned about the joy that comes with God's gift of salvation.

Presentation

1. Show the shoebox. **When have you gone to a store to buy new shoes? How did a salesperson help you?** Let children respond. **Dwight L. Moody was a successful shoe salesman in Boston, but one day his shoe sales didn't go as planned.**

2. **Dwight grew up in a very poor family. Dwight hated being poor and was determined to become rich. When he was 17 years old, he went to live with his uncle Samuel in Boston. He worked in his uncle's shoe store. Soon Dwight was making a lot of money because he was one of the best shoe salesmen around. Dwight's schoolteacher, Mr. Kimball, visited Dwight at the shoe store. Dwight thought his teacher had come to buy shoes. But Mr. Kimball did more than that—right there in the store he invited Dwight to become a member of God's family! Dwight did. He said he felt a new kind of happiness and love and everything was different. Now Dwight knew that true joy came from being a part of God's family! Dwight didn't want to keep his joy a secret. He went back home to visit his family to tell them about Jesus too. And for the rest of his life, Dwight spent most of his time telling people about Jesus and the joy that comes from being a Christian.**

Conclusion
Read Habakkuk 3:18 aloud. **How did Dwight Moody show he was joyful to know Jesus?** (He wanted to tell his family and other people about Jesus.) **Let's thank God for His gift of salvation.** Lead children in prayer.

Discussion Questions

1. **What are some reasons we have to "be joyful in God"? What are some reasons we have for being thankful to God?**

2. **What are some of the ways people hear about God's gift of salvation and the joy it brings?** (Friends tell them. They go to church. They read the Bible.)

3. **The Bible tells us God is joyful when we become a part of His family. Why?** (He loves us and wants us to be part of His family.)

4. **When we hear about God and accept God's gift of salvation by becoming members of God's family, we experience joy. Why?** (Our sins are forgiven by God. We can have eternal life. We know God loves us.) Talk with interested children about becoming members of God's family (see "Leading a Child to Christ" on p. 8).

Additional Information for Older Children

Dwight Moody became known as a man who tried to honor and obey God in all his actions. Dwight traveled all over America and England to preach about Jesus. Many people learned about Jesus through his preaching. People today still learn about Jesus from organizations Dwight helped to start, such as the Moody Bible Institute and Moody Publishers in Chicago.

Paid in Full

Becoming a Christian is more than knowing facts about God. God invites each of us to choose to belong to God's family and accept Jesus' love.

The wages of sin is death, but the gift of God is eternal life in Christ Jesus our Lord.

Romans 6:23

Materials

- Bible with a bookmark at Romans 6:23
- large sheet of paper or whiteboard
- marker
- calculator
- blank check
- pen

Introduction

God wants us to be part of His family so much He made it possible for us to receive His love and forgiveness for the wrong things we do. Let's find out how Jesus paid for our sins.

Presentation

1. **If we were to owe money for the wrong actions we've done, we would probably owe a lot of money. Ask children to name wrong actions.** (lying, stealing, cheating, fighting, etc.) As you list each wrong action on the paper or whiteboard, have the class decide on a dollar amount as penalty, or punishment, for each action (for example, $100 for lying), and write this amount next to the action. Ask a volunteer to add the amounts on the calculator and announce total to class. *(Optional: Depending on the age of your group, you may want to add the amounts on the calculator yourself.)*

2. **If someone loved you enough, that person could pay what you owe for your wrong actions by writing a check for the full amount.** Write out a check for the total amount, leaving the "to" and "from" portions blank.

Conclusion

The good news we read in the Bible is that the amount or punishment owed for our sin has been completely paid by Jesus, God's Son. Read Romans 6:23 aloud. **When Jesus died on the cross, He made it possible for our sins to be paid in full so that we can be part of God's family. What a great gift He gave us!** Complete the check, making the check out to "God," signing it from "Jesus," and writing "For _____'s (your name) sin" in the check memo portion. Lead the children in prayer, thanking God for His gift of salvation.

Discussion Questions

1. **How does doing wrong usually make a person feel?**

2. **How can asking God to forgive our sins help us?** (God promises to give us forgiveness and make us members of His family.)

3. **How do we know God's love is big enough to forgive all the wrong things we and others do?** (The Bible tells us so. God always keeps His promises.)

4. **How have you learned about God's love for you?** (from reading God's Word, from people who show God's love to others)

Signs of Change
God's gift of salvation can't be earned!

Materials
- Bible with a bookmark at Ephesians 2:8–9
- a variety of signs or fliers (For Sale, Beware of Dog, No Trespassing, advertising fliers, etc.)

Introduction
Because God's love for us is so great, He wants us to accept His free gift of salvation. A long time ago, a man named Martin Luther wanted to make sure everyone heard the good news about salvation. Let's find out what he did.

Presentation

1. One at a time, display and discuss the various signs you brought. **What does this sign tell you?** Volunteers can answer. Explain the signs as needed.

2. **Signs help people by giving them information they need. What are some other ways to give people information?** (television, radio, bulletin boards, Internet, and email)

3. **On October 31, 1517, Martin Luther nailed to a church door in Germany a paper that was like a sign. This paper explained that God's Word teaches that people do not need to buy God's gift of salvation by paying money to a priest.** (The people has been mistaken, thinking they had to buy their salvation.) When people realized a believer is forgiven by faith alone and a believer needs no other priest than Christ (see Hebrews 10:19–22), many of them stopped trying to buy salvation and simply asked God for His great gift! Today many people remember Martin Luther's actions on a day called Reformation Day. *Reformation* means to improve something, or to make right something that has been wrong.

Conclusion
Read Ephesians 2:8–9 aloud. **What do these verses say God gives us?** (salvation) **What does it mean to have faith?** (to trust and believe that God's Word is true and Jesus died and rose again to pay for our sins) Pray, thanking God for His free gift of salvation through Jesus. Talk with interested children about becoming members of God's family (see "Leading a Child to Christ" on p. 8).

Discussion Questions

1. **Grace is love and kindness shown to someone who doesn't deserve it. What does Ephesians 2:8–9 say about grace?** (We are saved because of God's grace.)

2. **Why can't we boast or brag about being saved?** (We are only saved when we believe in Jesus' death for our sins, not because of any good actions we have done.)

3. **Why is salvation described as a gift from God?** (It is free. There is nothing we can do to earn it. He gives it to us because He loves us.)

Additional Information for Older Children

Martin Luther's writings spread quickly. Here's why: Although Martin Luther wrote his paper in Latin, which many people didn't understand, his writing was later translated into German, a language that most people in his country understood. Then many people were able to read his writings. About the same time, the printing press was invented by Johannes Gutenberg in a nearby town. Thousands of copies of Luther's writings were printed. These copies were given out all over Europe. The good news of God's free gift of salvation traveled all over Europe and beyond!

Care for Foster Children

Sharing what you have can show your love for God and bring kindness to many people.

> ## Share with the Lord's people who are in need. Practice hospitality.
> Romans 12:13

Materials

- Bible with a bookmark at Romans 12:13
- food wrapper or bag from a fast-food restaurant

Introduction

We can bring kindness to many people when we share what we have. As we learn about one person who shared, think about how you can show God's love by sharing and bringing kindness to others.

Presentation

1. Show the food wrapper or bag. **What do you know about the place where I got this?** Accept responses. **Truett Cathy is one person who started a fast-food restaurant.**

2. **When he was a young man, Truett Cathy had a dream of owning a restaurant. He worked hard and saved his money. In 1946 Truett and his brother opened their first restaurant. Eventually, Truett started a chain of fast-food restaurants called Chick-fil-A. Chick-fil-A restaurants became very popular, and soon Truett was rich. Some rich people spend their money on big houses or new cars. But Truett loved God and believed the Bible verse says that it is better "to give than to receive" (Acts 20:35). Truett chose to spend his money helping children in foster care—children who have to live away from their parents because their parents can't take care of them. Many times children in foster care don't even get to keep living with their brothers and sisters. Truett felt sorry for these children, so he used his money to build foster homes where brothers and sisters could live together. Foster parents also live in the homes, so the children have a safe place to live and grow. Foster children in these homes are loved and cared for.**

Conclusion

Read Romans 12:13 aloud. **How did Truett Cathy obey this verse? How do you think his actions made a difference in other people's lives?** Children can share their ideas. **It pleases God when the members of His family are kind and share what they have with others.** Lead children in prayer, asking for God's help to find opportunities to be kind and share with others. Talk with interested children about becoming members of God's family (see "Leading a Child to Christ" on p. 8).

Discussion Questions

1. **What do you think are some good reasons for obeying Romans 12:13?** (to show God's love, to show that we thank God for His love)

2. **What are some things needed by people you know?**

3. **What can you share with others?** (clothes, friendship, knowledge of God's love)

Additional Information for Older Children

In addition to sharing money to help foster children, Truett Cathy gave money to Chick-fil-A workers who wanted to go to college. Since 1973 the company has given more than $36 million to help their workers go to college.

Gifts to Grow By

God can do great things with our gifts to Him.

Materials
- Bible with a bookmark at 1 Timothy 6:18
- popcorn kernels
- measuring cup
- popcorn maker
- large bowl
- serving bowls
- napkins
- salt *(optional)*

Introduction
Our gifts to God can be used by Him in many ways. Even small gifts of love and time can make a big difference. Let's look at something that starts out small and grows to be big!

Presentation
1. Pour popcorn kernels into the measuring cup until they measure half a cup (or the measurement appropriate for your popcorn maker). Ask a volunteer to look at the measuring cup and tell how much corn is in the cup.

2. **What happens to these popcorn kernels when they are heated?** (They pop. They get bigger.) Invite children to tell how much corn they think will be popped from the half cup of kernels.

3. Pop the popcorn and measure it. *(Optional: Ask Discussion Questions while waiting for the kernels to pop.)* Children can compare their predictions with the actual number of cups of popped corn.

4. Serve popcorn to the children. *(Optional: Children can sprinkle salt on the popcorn.)*

Conclusion
Sometimes we think our gifts to God are small and won't make much of a difference. But even our small gifts can be used by God in great ways. Listen to 1 Timothy 6:18 to find out some ways we can give to God. Read the verse aloud. **What does this verse say we can give to others? How are our right actions a gift to God?** (Our right actions show love for God and help others learn about Him.) Lead the children in prayer, asking God to show us ways to give to Him and to others.

Discussion Questions

1. **What are some other things that start out small and get bigger?** (cookies until they're baked, babies until they grow to be adults, plant and tree seeds until they're planted and watered)

2. **In what ways might kids your age give to God?** (give time to help others, donate our possessions that are needed by others) Tell the children about ways the people in your church give to others to show love for God.

3. **What is one way you can give to God?**

Good Soup

Listening to others and treating them fairly are ways to show God's goodness.

Materials
- Bible with a bookmark at Zechariah 7:9
- can of soup

Introduction

God's goodness shows in our lives when we listen to others and treat them fairly. Let's find out how one man showed God's goodness in the way he treated others.

> **This is what the LORD Almighty said: "Administer true justice; show mercy and compassion to one another."**
>
> Zechariah 7:9

Presentation

1. Show the can of soup. **When do you like to eat soup? What kinds of soup do you like best?** Invite responses. **One man was not happy when he saw some poor-tasting soup that was being served in his city.**

2. **Charles Tindley was born as a slave, just a few years before Abraham Lincoln set the slaves free. When he grew up, Charles became the pastor of a church in the city of Philadelphia. Charles worried about some poor people who lived on the streets instead of in homes. He wanted to treat them in good ways, and he wanted to teach them about Jesus. One day Charles went to a kitchen where poor people were given soup and bread to eat. But when Charles looked at the food, he saw that the soup was very watery and the bread was stale. Charles felt sorry for the people and wanted them to receive better food. The next Sunday, Charles told his congregation they were going to help the poor people in their city. The church members cooked good, healthy food and welcomed the poor people into their church. Charles often talked to the poor people and showed how much he cared about them. Many of these people considered Charles their own pastor because he cared enough to listen to them and treat them in good ways.**

Conclusion

Read Zechariah 7:9 aloud. **When we "administer true justice," it means we treat others fairly. What else does this verse say God wants us to do?** Children can respond. **How did Charles Tindley show mercy and compassion to others?** (He helped poor people have good food to eat.) Lead the children in prayer, asking God to help them listen to others and treat others fairly.

Discussion Questions

1. **When are some times it might be hard for you to listen to others? How does listening to someone help a person know the best ways to help?** (By listening, a person can learn what is really needed and what to pray for.)

2. **What does it mean to treat other people fairly?** (Respect each person. Care for all people in the same way you care for the people you like most.) **What can you do to treat your brother or sister more fairly? How about kids at school?**

3. **How can listening to others and treating them fairly help them see God's goodness?** (It shows them God thinks each person is important.)

4. **What are some other ways that your actions can show God's goodness?**

Additional Information for Older Children

When Charles Tindley was a boy, his father was very poor, so Charles worked for farmers by doing chores. As he grew up, he had to work so much he was unable to go to school. But Charles wanted to learn to read. He collected newspaper pages other people had thrown away, and he slowly taught himself how to read. Then Charles was able to read the only book he had—the Bible.

Homes for the Homeless

Kindness is doing good without expecting anything in return.

Materials
- Bible with a bookmark at 1 Thessalonians 3:12
- hammer and other construction tools

Introduction
When we do good without expecting anything in return, we are showing kindness. Let's look at a way some people work hard to show kindness, even though they don't get paid any money for it.

Presentation

1. Show the construction tools. **What do people use these tools for?** Volunteers can answer. **Carpenters who build furniture and houses usually get paid for their work. But some people who work as carpenters don't get paid at all! These people work for an organization called Habitat for Humanity.** *Habitat* **is a word that means "the place where someone lives."** *Humanity* **is a word that means "people." What do you think people who work for Habitat for Humanity might do?** (build homes for people who don't have a good place to live)

2. **One man who worked for Habitat for Humanity used to be the president of the United States. His name is Jimmy Carter. After a new president was elected, President Carter could have looked for a job to earn lots of money. But instead, because he loved God and wanted to show God's love to others, he decided to spend some of his time working for Habitat for Humanity. Jimmy Carter and the other people who help Habitat for Humanity don't get any pay in return for building houses for people. They build houses because they want to show kindness to others in need.**

Conclusion
Read 1 Thessalonians 3:12 aloud. **How does this verse describe how we should show love? Something overflows when there's so much of it that it won't stay in one place. It spreads out everywhere! How does Jimmy Carter's kindness show God's love?** (He helps others without expecting to get money or anything else in return.) Pray, asking God to help your children find ways to be kind to others.

Discussion Questions

1. **What are some ways to show kindness to others without expecting anything in return?** (help a younger brother or sister, donate items to a homeless shelter)

2. **When has someone been kind to you? What did that person do? Why do you think that person chose to be kind?**

3. **When have you been kind to another person? What happened as a result of your kindness?**

Additional Information for Older Children

In 1981 the United States had a new president. Even though Jimmy Carter wasn't the president anymore, he and his wife, Rosalynn, still wanted to help people all over the world. They started the Carter Center, a nonprofit organization to help people be peaceful and treat others fairly. Through the years, the Carter Center has worked with many different countries to improve the way the people in those countries live. In 1999 Jimmy and Rosalynn Carter were presented with a very important award, the Presidential Medal of Freedom.

School Uniforms

Look for ways to be kind to and care for others.

Materials
- Bible with a bookmark at Matthew 5:7
- uniform from a school or sports team

> **Blessed are the merciful, for they will be shown mercy.**
>
> Matthew 5:7

Introduction
It is important to always look for opportunities in which we can be kind to and care for others. Let's find out some ways one woman found to be kind to and care for others.

Presentation

1. Show the uniform. *(Optional: A volunteer could wear the uniform.)* **When do kids your age wear uniforms?** Children can respond. **In the early 1900s, school children in China wore uniforms. Schools even had contests to see which school had the best uniform. The children in one school, however, were embarrassed because they did not have uniforms like other children. This school was so poor, the teachers could hardly buy school supplies. And because the children in the school were orphans (their parents were no longer alive), they couldn't afford to buy uniforms.**

2. **Grace Chang was a missionary teacher at this school. She cared for the children at the school so much she decided to help them get uniforms. Grace planned to use her sewing machine to make the uniforms, but she didn't have any cloth! Grace prayed and asked God to help her. God answered Grace's prayer. Soon another missionary gave her some cloth, and Grace started sewing uniforms for the children. Then Grace got women in a nearby village to help make cloth shoes for all the children. (At that time, Chinese children typically wore cloth shoes.) Soon the jackets, skirts, and even the shoes were ready. The children excitedly wore their uniforms to school. And when they won the contest for the best uniform, the children were even more pleased!**

Conclusion
Read Matthew 5:7 aloud. **When we show mercy to others, it means we are kind to them—even when they don't deserve it. How did Grace Chang show mercy and kindness to others?** Accept responses. **Let's ask God to help us find ways to be kind and care for others this week.** Close in prayer.

Discussion Questions

1. Grace Chang used her sewing machine to be kind to others. What could you use to be kind to someone?

2. When has someone been kind to you? Why do you think that person chose to be kind? How did you feel as a result of that kindness?

3. Who are some people you could be kind to and care for this week?

Additional Information for Older Children

Grace Chang trusted that God would help her show kindness to others. Once, another missionary became ill and needed someone to take her home to the United States. Grace was asked to help her, but neither woman had any money for the boat ride! Grace prayed and prayed and then felt sure God wanted her to borrow money from a bank. Even though Grace had nothing to give the bank in return, the bank manager loaned her the money!

Service with a Smile

Be ready to serve others with a gentle attitude.

Materials
- Bible with a bookmark at Galatians 5:13
- scrub brush
- bucket

Introduction
Being ready to serve others with a gentle attitude helps us show God's love. Let's find out how someone showed God's love with a scrub brush.

Presentation
1. Show the scrub brush and bucket. **When have you used a scrub brush or bucket?** Volunteers can answer. **Some people don't like to wash floors or cars, because they think it's not very important work. In 1895 a woman named Amy Carmichael had to scrub something dirty to show what it meant to serve others.**

2. **Amy had gone to India as a missionary. She noticed that many children needed a safe place to live. Some of these children came to live with Amy. Soon Amy was taking care of 17 children! Sometimes Amy wondered if she had been right in giving up important work in other places to take care of the children. But Amy remembered that Jesus showed God's love by serving His disciples and washing their feet. Taking care of the children was valuable because it was a way she could serve others and show God's love!**

3. **One day a new woman came to help care for the children. Amy asked the woman to serve by washing the nursery floor. The woman refused because she wanted an easier, better job. So Amy took the bucket of soapy water and got down on her hands and knees and scrubbed the dirty floor. Because Amy was willing to do this hard work, she gently helped the woman learn how important it is to show God's love by serving others in whatever way is needed.**

Conclusion
Read Galatians 5:13 aloud. **What are some ways Amy Carmichael served others in love?** Children can respond. **Let's ask God to help us serve others with gentle attitudes.** Lead children in prayer.

Discussion Questions

1. **What do you think the verse means when it says to "serve" someone in love?** (be kind and gentle when we help, don't have a bossy or proud attitude, pay attention to the needs of others)

2. **What are some ways to serve others?** (get a glass of water for someone who is sitting down resting, set the table without being asked, help your mom by taking care of younger brothers or sisters while she cooks dinner, make a card for someone who is sick)

3. **What can you do this week to serve others at school? At home? On the playground?**

Additional Information for Older Children

Amy Carmichael broke her leg when she was older. Her leg didn't heal correctly, so she couldn't walk for the rest of her life. Instead of being angry she couldn't do the things she had done before, Amy still served others by writing many books that helped people learn more about missionaries and about God's love for people all over the world.

Talented People

Use the talents God gave you to serve others.

Materials
- Bible with bookmarks at Psalm 145:10 and 1 Peter 4:10
- large sheet of paper or whiteboard
- marker
- paper, markers *(optional)*

> **Each of you should use whatever gift you have received to serve others.**
>
> 1 Peter 4:10

Preparation
In the middle of the large sheet of paper or whiteboard, vertically print the word *talents*, leaving space between each letter.

Introduction
Each of us can use the talents God gave us to do good things for others. Let's talk about different talents and how we can use them in ways that please God.

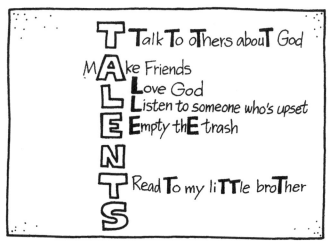

Presentation
1. Show the paper or whiteboard. **Let's make a kind of acrostic to see how many talents we can think of that begin with or use each letter of the word *talents*. What are some things that kids your age like to do or are good at?** Print the ideas next to the appropriate letters. *(Optional: Give paper and markers to each child and ask them to make individual acrostics using their names and talents.)*

2. **Some psalms are written like acrostics also. Psalm 145 is called an alphabet acrostic because in the Hebrew language the verses of the psalm begin with the letters of the Hebrew alphabet in order. King David wrote this psalm a long time ago. In this psalm we can read a reason we have all been given special talents.** Read or ask a child to read Psalm 145:10. **Everything God made or does praises Him. When we use our talents for Him, to help and serve others, it's a way of praising God.**

Conclusion

Read 1 Peter 4:10 aloud. **What does it mean. to serve others?** (to help them, to give them what they need) **What are some ways kids your age can serve others?** Pray, thanking God for the talents He's given us and asking for His help in finding ways to use our talents to help others.

Discussion Questions

1. **How has someone used a talent to help you?** (helped me learn to read, helped me make friends)

2. **What kinds of things do you enjoy doing? What are you good at doing?** (being friendly, playing soccer, reading, singing)

3. **When have you used a talent to serve others?**

Additional Information for Older Children

Read or ask an older child to read Romans 12:6–8 aloud. **What are some of the talents, or gifts, this verse describes?** Invite responses. **In this verse, the word** *gift* **comes from the Greek word** *charismata* (kah-rees-MAH-tah). **This word tells us these gifts are special, freely given by God to meet the needs of His family.**

Traveling School

Goodness includes using what God gives you to help others.

Materials

- Bible with a bookmark at 1 Peter 4:10
- peanuts (check for allergies)
- chickpeas, toothpicks for serving *(optional)*

> **Each of you should use whatever gift you have received to serve others.**
>
> 1 Peter 4:10

Introduction

Using what God gives us to help others is a big part of showing goodness. Let's find out how one man used what God had given him to help others.

Presentation

1. Show the peanuts. **What are some things people use peanuts for?** (to eat, to make peanut butter) **Before the early 1900s, few people grew peanuts because they didn't know how to use the peanuts. But a man named George Washington Carver believed God had given him a brain to help him discover how the peanut could be used. Dr. Carver discovered over 300 things that could be made from peanuts, including printer's ink, a milk substitute, face powder, soap, and candy.** (Note: If a child is allergic to peanuts, comment, **While some people are allergic to peanuts, there are other good uses for them besides eating them.**)

2. **Dr. Carver also discovered many things about the best ways to grow plants. And he didn't keep what he learned to himself! Dr. Carver used what he had learned about plants to help others. Dr. Carver and a friend got a horse and wagon and set up a portable school. They traveled to poor farms all over their county to teach African American farmers better ways to grow plants. He also taught them new ways to use the things they grew so that they could make money selling new products. Some people complained that Dr. Carver should make people pay to learn the things he was teaching. But Dr. Carver insisted that money was not important. Dr. Carver told people that it didn't matter how much money they had or how fancy their clothes were. He said that serving others was more important than money or clothes. In fact, in one of his jobs, Dr. Carver didn't accept a pay raise for 40 years! All that mattered to him was helping people.**

Conclusion

Read 1 Peter 4:10 aloud. **How did George Washington Carver show goodness and obey 1 Peter 4:10?** Lead the children in prayer, asking God to help them find good ways to help others.

Discussion Questions

1. Who is someone you know that shows goodness? What does that person do to show goodness?

2. What are some things you enjoy doing or are good at doing? How can you use these things to help others?

3. Who are some people you can help or serve this week?

Additional Information for Older Children

When Dr. Carver first began teaching people how to grow better crops, some of the farmers didn't believe what he said. So as part of his teaching, Dr. Carver would show them sample plants and patiently explain how to grow the plants. Sometimes Dr. Carver would even cook a good-tasting meal to show people how they could make food from their crops. *(Optional: Let volunteers taste chickpeas [garbanzo beans], one of the foods Dr. Carver taught others to eat.)*

Will Work for Free
Humble and gentle attitudes help us not to look down on others.

Materials
- Bible with a bookmark at Philippians 2:3
- money

> **Do nothing out of selfish ambition or vain conceit. Rather, in humility value others above yourselves.**
>
> Philippians 2:3

Introduction
When we have humble and gentle attitudes, we won't look down on others. Let's find out how one man showed a humble and gentle attitude.

Presentation
1. Show the money. **What are some ways people get money? Why do you think some people want to have lots of money?** Children can share their ideas. **When do you think someone might NOT want to have lots of money? In the country of Japan, a man by the name of Toyohiko** (toh-yoh-HEE-koh) **Kagawa** (kah-GAH-wah) **chose not to be paid a lot of money for his hard work.**

2. **Kagawa lived in a shack in the poor part of his town. He lived there so that he could help the other people who lived there learn about Jesus. While Mr. Kagawa was living in this part of town, a terrible earthquake destroyed most of the city. An important city leader told Mr. Kagawa that the city needed him to help people rebuild their homes, to make sure people had food to eat and water to drink, and to help the poor people find good jobs. The official said, "This job pays a good salary, and you will be given a car." Mr. Kagawa surprised the official when he said that he would be glad to do the job, but he would not take money or a car. Instead, Mr. Kagawa asked that his salary be used to help poor people. Mr. Kagawa's actions showed that he was humble. He believed the needs of poor people were just as important as his own needs.**

Conclusion
Read Philippians 2:3 aloud. **How did Mr. Kagawa show he was humble?** (He lived in a small house. He asked that poor people be helped with the money he worked for.) Lead the children in prayer, asking God to help them have humble and gentle attitudes.

Discussion Questions

1. **What are some ways to describe a person who is humble?** (cares about others, remembers that other people are important, wants to do what is best for other people)

2. **How do you feel when someone acts like he or she is better than you are? How would you want to be treated instead?**

3. **What are some things you could do to show a humble and gentle attitude?** (let others go first, don't act better than everyone else, listen carefully when others speak)

4. **When we have humble attitudes, we don't spend our time comparing ourselves to others. What should we think about instead?** (ways to love God and others, how we can help others)

Additional Information for Older Children

A teacher, poet, and scientist, Mr. Kagawa wrote 150 books. He was known to repeat three prayers: "Father, forgive"; "God, let me live to serve"; and "O God, make me like Christ." These prayers showed how much Mr. Kagawa loved God and how much he wanted to obey God by helping others.

Thankfulness

An Itchy Situation
God's gift of joy can help us be thankful in any situation.

Sing and make music from your heart to the Lord, always giving thanks to God the Father for everything, in the name of our Lord Jesus Christ.

Ephesians 5:19–20

Materials
- Bible with a bookmark at Ephesians 5:19–20
- anti-itch cream
- cotton swabs *(optional)*

Introduction
We can be thankful in any situation because of the joy God gives to us. Let's find out about an unusual situation in which two women found that they could be thankful.

Presentation

1. Show the anti-itch cream. *(Optional: Use cotton swabs to dab a small amount of cream on the hands of volunteers. Be aware of any allergies.)* **When might someone need an anti-itch cream?** Children can respond. **Many years ago, during World War II, a woman named Corrie ten Boom and her sister, Betsy, could have used a cream like this.**

2. **Corrie and Betsy were living in a prison camp. They had been arrested because they had helped Jewish people hide from the Nazis. The two sisters worked hard all day and slept in a crowded, smelly room at night. Corrie often felt like complaining—especially because the room in which they slept was full of fleas. Fleas hopped everywhere. Fleas even lived in the straw the women had to sleep on. The itching was awful! Betsy reminded Corrie that God could do good things in any situation. They decided to be thankful and even thanked God for the fleas. But they must have wondered how God could make something good happen in their terrible situation.Each night Corrie and Betsy read the Bible aloud to the other women in the room. At first, they posted lookouts to keep watch for the guards, because anyone caught with a Bible would certainly be killed! But one day they found out that no guards ever came to their room—because of all the fleas! Corrie and Betsy thanked God because the fleas made it easier to read the Bible and teach others about God's love.**

Conclusion

Read Ephesians 5:19–20 aloud. **What do these verses say about thanking God? Why do you think Corrie and Betsy ten Boom were able to thank God, even in a very bad situation?** (They knew God would always be with them and help them.) **God gives us good things and loves us, even when we are having hard times.** Invite the children to pray, telling God things they are thankful for.

Discussion Questions

1. **When are some times that it is hard to thank God? Why?**

2. **What could you give thanks for when you have a bad day at school?** (ability to read, a school to attend) **What can you give thanks for when you are sick?** (a bed to rest in)

3. **What are some ways to show God's gift of joy?** (singing or playing an instrument in a song of praise, telling others about God)

Additional Information for Older Children

Corrie, Betsy, and the other members of their family were arrested by the Nazis for hiding Jewish people in their home. On the top floor of their house, a small secret room was built behind Corrie's bedroom. In that tiny room, they hid Jewish people. Even though all of Corrie and Betsy's family were arrested, none of the Jewish people they hid were ever found. After World War II ended, Corrie wrote many books. One book, *The Hiding Place*, is about her family's adventures hiding Jewish people from the Nazis.

Cornucopia of Thanks
Give thanks to God for His care for us.

Materials
- Bible with a bookmark at Exodus 15:2
- cornucopia or large basket
- magazine pictures of good things God has given us (food, family, friends, church, parks, school, nature items—1 picture for each child, including several examples from each category)

Preparation
Place the pictures in the cornucopia or large basket.

Introduction
As we learn about God, we discover the many wonderful ways He cares for us. God's care for us is something we can celebrate and thank Him for! Let's find out some of the gifts He gives us.

Presentation
1. Ask a volunteer to take a picture from the cornucopia or basket, identifying the picture for the entire group. What is one thing about this picture that makes you want to thank God? Repeat, using a different volunteer for each picture.

2. At your signal, have children group themselves into categories according to their pictures. Repeat as time allows, having children select new pictures.

3. **What are some of the things people do to show their thankfulness?** (say "thank you," write thank-you notes) **In several countries around the world, such as the United States, Canada, Brazil, and Argentina, Thanksgiving Day is celebrated to thank God for the good things He gives.** (Optional: If your children celebrate Thanksgiving, invite volunteers to tell about their family celebrations.)

Conclusion

Read Exodus 15:2 aloud. **What are some of the ways we can praise God for the good things He gives us?** (We can sing songs that thank God, read God's Word, and pray to God.) Pray, thanking God for His loving care and the good things He has given us.

Discussion Questions

1. **What are some ways God cares for your family? For what would you like to thank God?**

2. **How can you show God that you are thankful for His love and care?** (name the things you are thankful for when you pray, write God a thank-you prayer, sing praise songs to Him)

3. **What are some ways to give thanks to God?** (sing Him a song of thanks, tell Him what you are thankful for when you pray) **What is your favorite way to thank God?**

Additional Information for Older Children

The United States and Canada celebrate Thanksgiving Day in similar ways but on different days. In Canada, Thanksgiving Day is celebrated on the second Monday in October. Canada's Parliament, in 1957, decreed it should be "a day of general thanksgiving to almighty God for the bountiful harvest with which Canada has been blessed." In the United States, Thanksgiving Day is celebrated on the fourth Thursday in November. President Abraham Lincoln issued a proclamation in 1863 to set this day aside "as a day of Thanksgiving and Praise to our beneficent Father."

Making Music

We can thank God for all things and in all circumstances because we know He is always with us.

Materials

- Bible with a bookmark at Ephesians 5:19–20
- 6 identical clear water glasses
- pitcher of water
- spoon

> Sing and make music from your heart to the Lord, always giving thanks to God the Father for everything, in the name of our Lord Jesus Christ.
>
> Ephesians 5:19–20

Preparation

Fill the glasses with water as shown in the sketch.

Introduction

We all have times or situations that make us feel sad or happy. Because we know God is good. and always with us, we can thank God for all things. Let's try a fun way to give thanks to God.

Presentation

1. Demonstrate how to play musical notes by gently tapping the glasses with the spoon. Point out to the children that different amounts of water in the glasses cause dif erent notes. *(Optional: Invite volunteers to experiment with tapping the glasses.)*

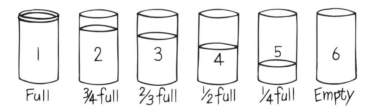

1 Full   2 ¾ full   3 ⅔ full   4 ½ full   5 ¼ full   6 Empty

2. **It's fun to make up our own music with these glasses. Listen to Ephesians 5:19–20 to see what it says about music.** Read the verses aloud. **Making music in our hearts means we're so glad and thankful; our prayers to God are like songs. Many of the songs we sing in church are prayers of thankfulness and praise to God.**

3. Choose a phrase from the verses, such as "giving thanks to God the Father" or "Sing and make music from your heart" and tap the glasses as you say or sing the words. Invite the children to say or sing the words with you. *(Optional: Invite several children to tap the glasses for these or other phrases from the verses.)*

Conclusion

Lead the children in a prayer of thanks to God.

Discussion Questions

1. **What are some ways of giving thanks to God?** (saying or writing prayers)

2. **What are some things you are thankful for?**

3. **When might you and your family give thanks to God at home?**

Offering It All

Our offerings of love, time, abilities, and money are ways we show our thankfulness to God.

Materials
- Bible with a bookmark at 1 Chronicles 16:29
- objects used by your church to collect offerings (boxes, bags, plates, tithe envelopes, banks, etc.)
- large bag
- blindfold
- children's Bible dictionaries *(optional)*

Preparation
Place in the bag the objects used to collect offerings.

Introduction
An offering is anything we give to show love for God. We can give offerings of love, time, abilities, and money to show our thankfulness to God. In the Old Testament, people gave many different types of offerings to God too. Let's look at different ways to give to God.

Presentation
1. Invite a volunteer to wear the blindfold. Then take one object from the bag, hand it to the blindfolded volunteer and ask him or her to identify the object. What is this object used for? Let the volunteer respond. Repeat, using a different volunteer for each object.

2. **We use all these objects in our church to collect offerings.** Explain the use of the objects to the children as needed. **What are some other ways people give to show their love and thankfulness to God?** (bring canned foods, give used clothes, volunteer time to help or teach others at church, sing in the choir)

3. **In Old Testament times, people gave different kinds of offerings too. They gave animals, grains, oil, fruits, and vegetables. God's people brought their offerings to the tabernacle and later to the temple—the places where the people gath-ered to worship God. The offerings were burned at a special place called an altar. These offerings were called sacrifices.** *(Optional: Read, or ask an older child to read, Leviticus 1:1–2; 2:1–2; 3:1 aloud.)* **Some of the offerings showed God the people were sorry for sinning; others showed they wanted to love and obey God and were thankful for His good gifts to them.**

Conclusion

The Bible tells us to give offerings to God. Read 1 Chronicles 16:29 aloud. **Unlike people in Old Testament times, we don't have to make offerings because of sin. Jesus died and rose again to pay for ALL our sins. His sacrifice was the most important offering ever. Now we bring offerings to show our praise to God.** Pray, thanking God for the good things He gives us.

Discussion Questions

1. **What kinds of offerings can you give to God?** (money, time helping others, love for God and others, singing songs of praise)

2. **What attitude should we have when we give offerings to God?** (an attitude of thankfulness, a happy and willing attitude that shows we are glad to give to God because we love Him and want to help the people He loves)

3. **When have you or your family given money or other things you own to show thankfulness to God?** (given books to a missionary family, given money to church to help other people learn about God)

4. **Why is it important to give offerings to God?** (helps us remember God's gifts to us)

Additional Information for Older Children

Provide several children's Bible dictionaries. Invite children to read information about the different types of offerings described in the Old Testament: burnt offerings, grain offerings, fellowship offerings, sin offerings, and guilt offerings.

Songs of Joy

God's gifts to us bring joy and cause our thankfulness to overflow.

The Lord is my strength and my shield; my heart trusts in him, and he helps me. My heart leaps for joy, and with my song I praise him.

Psalm 28:7

Materials
- Bible with a bookmark at Psalm 28:7
- hymnal
- bookmarks

Introduction

Remembering God's gifts to us helps us be joyful and want to thank God. Let's look at a book written by people whose thankfulness to God couldn't help but show.

Presentation

1. Open the hymnal and show it to the children. **What is in this book? How are books like this used?** Volunteers can respond. **Hymnals are books of songs about God. These songs were written by many different people who loved God and wanted others to love Him too. One hymn writer's name was Frances Crosby. (She is often called by the nickname Fanny.)**

2. **Frances Crosby was born in New York in 1820. When Frances was only six weeks old, she became sick and** eventually became blind. Then shortly after Frances became blind, her father died and her family became very poor. In spite of the bad things that happened to her, Frances Crosby didn't feel sorry for herself. When she grew up, Frances became a teacher at a school for the blind. She also was a concert singer and played the piano and the harp. And Frances wrote songs, thousands of them! During her lifetime, Frances Crosby wrote over 8,000 songs and poems—and many of them were written to show her love and thankfulness to God.

Conclusion

Read Psalm 28:7 aloud. **Among the good gifts God gave Frances Crosby were some special talents. What were some of her talents?** (Frances could play the piano and harp. She could sing well and write songs. She was a teacher.) **How did Frances use her gifts to show her thanks to God?** (She wrote and sang songs about God. She taught others about God.) Lead the children in prayer, thanking God for His gifts to them.

Discussion Questions

1. **What are some of the good gifts God gives us?** (people who love us, food, clothing, forgiveness of sins, talents)

2. **What can you do to thank God for these gifts?** (We can tell Him words of praise and thanks, tell other people how great He is, sing songs of thankfulness to Him, and use the gifts to praise Him.)

3. **The best gift God ever gave us was His Son, Jesus. Jesus makes it possible for us to become members of God's family. What are some ways to show we are thankful for Jesus?** (say prayers of thanks to God, sing songs about Jesus) Talk with interested children about becoming members of God's family (see "Leading a Child to Christ" on p. 8).

Additional Information for Older Children

In a church hymnal, use bookmarks to mark several hymns written by Frances (Fanny) Crosby. Her hymns include "To God Be the Glory," "Blessed Assurance," "I Am Thine, O Lord," "Praise Him! Praise Him!," and "Redeemed." Volunteers can find and read or sing the marked hymn. **What do these hymns talk about? What did Frances Crosby want to thank God for? What words or phrases remind you of being happy or joyful?**

Index

Bible Verse

Biography